WWII BATTLE TRIVIA FOR KIDS

FASCINATING FACTS ABOUT THE BIGGEST BATTLES, INVASIONS, AND VICTORIES OF WORLD WAR II

BRETTE SEMBER

T0040101

BLOOM BOOKS FOR YOUNG READERS

Published by:
Bloom Books for Young Readers,
an imprint of Ulysses Press
PO Box 3440
Berkeley, CA 94703
www.ulyssespress.com

ISBN: 978-1-64604-182-4
Library of Congress Control Number: 2021931324

Printed in the United States by Kingery Printing Company
10 9 8 7 6 5 4 3 2

Acquisitions editor: Claire Sielaff
Managing editor: Claire Chun
Project editor: Ashten Evans
Editor: Scott Calamar
Proofreader: Barbara Schultz
Cover design: Rebecca Lown
Interior design: what!design @ whatweb.com
Interior photographs: see page 144
Production: Jake Flaherty, Yesenia Garcia-Lopez

This book is dedicated to my grandfather,
Private First Class Raymond McWhorter,
who served in the 287th QM Refrigeration Company
in Central Europe from January 1943 to January 1946.
He earned the World War II Victory Medal, the American
Defense Service Medal, the European-African-Middle
Eastern Campaign Medal, and a Good Conduct Medal.
Thank you for your service, Grampa. We love and miss you.

CONTENTS

INTRODUCTION 1

WWII TIMELINE 4

BATTLEFIELD LIFE 7

How young was the youngest American to fight in the war? 8

What did battlefield soldiers use for toilet paper? 8

Why did Japanese soldiers wear special belts as part of their uniform? 8

What was the standard-issue rifle used by the German infantry
in World War II? 8

Which country lost the most people in World War II? 9

How much weight did the average US soldier carry in battle? 9

What was one of the most common injuries in the war that had
nothing to do with bullets or bombs? 10

What battle cry did the Soviet soldiers often shout on the battlefield? 10

Which Japanese soldier remained at war the longest? 10

What did troops eat on the front lines? 11

For American sailors on ships in the Atlantic, what did the order
"general quarters" mean? 12

How many U-boats did the Germans use during World War II? 12

What luxury did American submarines have? 12

What was the Momsen lung? 12

Why did the air in submarines smell so bad during the war? 13

What was the most popular dish at the Honolulu USO? 14

What luxury did US hospital ships have? 14

What was the largest cause of death in World War II? 15

How many deceased American soldiers' bodies were never
returned home after the war? 15

How did Monopoly games help some soldiers escape? 15

What was a battlefield cross? 16

Who was named a Crow Tribe war chief for his acts during the war? 16

What were banzai attacks? 17

What was it like when a battleship fired at the enemy? 17

Which country suffered the highest percentage loss of its population
in the war? 17

How many naval mines were laid during the war? 18

How much were American soldiers paid during the war? 18

What was an elephant gun? 18

What was *Englandspiel*? 18

What was the Flying Fortress? 19

What was a Little Katie? 19

What was a human torpedo? 20

How did decks of cards help American POWs? 20

Who were the Seabees? 20

What was the doodlebug? 20

How many prisoners of war were taken during World War II? 21

How much did the war cost? 21

What was in British RAF crews' survival kits? 21

What special footwear was issued to US airborne troops? 22

What was the Baka? 22

What did American troops read while on the battlefield? 22

What were Foo Fighters? 24

What were Jericho Trumpets? 24

What were the Para Dogs? 24

What was one of the biggest dangers facing pilots in the war? 24

What was the standard issue field coat for US soldiers in the war? 25

How many German generals died in the war? 25

How many American generals died in the war? 25

How did a Hungarian mathematician save the lives of many American air force men?... 26

Why did some troops eat steak and eggs for breakfast?............... 26

How did a bear travel with Polish troops during the war?.............. 27

What was unique about US General MacArthur's hat?................. 27

How did matchbooks impact the German army?..................... 27

How many men who served in the war later became president of the United States?... 28

1939.................................... 29

What was the first battle of World War II?.......................... 30

How did math result in the scuttle of a German ship?................ 30

Which wartime strategy memo was likely influenced by a famous author?.. 31

Who fought on skis in the war?.................................. 32

What was the first ship sunk in World War II?...................... 33

What was the Phony War?....................................... 33

Why did Germany attack Poland and start the war?.................. 33

Why did Britain order a million coffins in preparation for the war?........ 34

Although the United States remained neutral when the war began in 1939, what did the president urge Americans to do? 34

How many tanks did Germany send into Poland during the invasion? 34

Why did the Soviet Union invade Poland? 35

How successful was France at defending its ally Poland when it was invaded by the Germans? 35

How did Poland's military compare to Germany's? 35

How much of a defense did Poland mount when the Soviet Union attacked? 35

Why were the snakes in the London Zoo killed in 1939? 36

Why was Germany's invasion of Belgium and France postponed twice? 36

What action did France take during the Phony War?.................. 36

How badly were Finnish forces outnumbered by Soviet forces?........... 36

How was the British battleship *Royal Oak* sunk? 37

What was the Venlo Incident? 37

What was the name of the ship that fired the first shots of the war? 37

How did Germany capture Czechoslovakia without any warfare? 38

What was the Sausage War? 38

1940 41

How were balloons used to fight the war? 42

What was the shortest battle of World War II? 42

What does "blitzkrieg" mean in German? 42

How did old biplanes hold off the Italians? 43

How did the United States supply Britain with planes despite
a neutrality agreement? 43

Which fighter plane was developed in just 102 days? 44

How did the Germans sneak into France to occupy it? 45

Who was the only soldier who killed with a longbow during the war? 45

Which vehicle was inspired by a hurricane? 45

What were bomb cemeteries? 46

What was the Miracle at Dunkirk? 46

What was the cavity magnetron? 47

What popular vehicle was invented as America prepared for war? 47

What strategy did the Germans use to gain a foothold in Norway? 47

Where was the surrender ceremony held when France surrendered
to Germany? 48

What was Black Thursday? 48

How did the Germans use radio beams to target the British city
of Coventry? 48

Did an Axis commander ever nominate an Allied commander for
a medal? 49

When did Italy enter the war? 50

Why did Italy invade Greece? 50

How did the Norwegian royal family escape the Nazis? 50

What tactic did German U-boats use to evade detection by the British
in the Battle of the Atlantic? 50

Which medical invention saved thousands of lives during the war? 51

How did a British agent steal diamonds from underneath
the Nazis' noses? 51

Why did the British sink some French navy ships in French Algeria? 52

What was the Battle of Switzerland? 52

Which children's author crashed his plane in the war and survived? 54

Did the Germans ever fight in the Pacific Ocean? 54

What do today's Purple Hearts have to do with World War II? 54

1941 55

Who was the most decorated female veteran of World War II? 56

How did one sailor change the navy's segregation policy? 56

What was the last radio message from the *Bismarck*? 57

What were "wolf packs" during the Battle of the Atlantic? 58

How did a lack of fuel almost ruin a winning British strategy? 58

What were the Doolittle Raids? 59

How did radar almost prevent the bombing of Pearl Harbor? 59

What was the first military engagement between the US and
Germany? 59

How did artificial legs save a pilot's life? 60

Which Atlantic island nation did the United States occupy
during the war? 61

What was the Continuation War? 61

Why did Rommel wear goggles on his hat? 62

Why did the Blitz end? 62

What was the Afrika Korps? 63

Which sports fields did Iraqis use to fight the British in the war? 63

Which German victory convinced Hitler to stop using paratroopers
for sneak attacks? 63

How many horses did the Germans use when invading the
Soviet Union? 64

How did weather protect Moscow from invasion? 64

When did Hitler first order mass killings? 64

What was the first American ship sunk in the war? 65

What method of transportation helped the Japanese take Malaya? 65

When did Britain declare war on Japan? 65

How many Americans died in the attack on Pearl Harbor? 65

What was the first Japanese vessel sunk by the Americans in the war? 66

When did the draft begin in the United States for World War II? 67

Who was the only German POW to escape from Canada and rejoin the war? 67

How did Stalin's son end up in the hands of the Germans? 68

Who was Lady Death? 68

Which airman climbed out onto the wing of a plane during flight
to save it? 69

1942 71

Was United States land ever occupied by another country during
World War II? 72

What was the bloodiest battle in the entire history of the world? 73

Who were the *Malgré-nous*? 73

Which battle was fought against no one? 73

What was the secret to the Americans defeating Japan in the
Battle of Midway? 74

What did the saying "a man a mile" mean? 75

How difficult was it for reporters to take photos at the front lines? 75

What was V-mail? 75

Which submarine was always greeted with stacks of toilet paper,
toilet paper streamers, and toilet paper necklaces? 76

How did dogs serve in the war? 77

The crew of which ship survived in lifeboats for 20 days after their ship
was sunk? 78

How was a sailor saved by his mother during the Battle of
Guadalcanal? 78

When did the first Code Talkers begin their work in the war? 79

How many Japanese aircraft carriers were taken out during the
Battle of Midway? 81

What was Hitler's plan for the citizens of Stalingrad? 81

What was the strategy of island-hopping? 81

What was the Tokyo Express? 81

Why were marines based in Guadalcanal given machetes? 82

Which Japanese general drowned retreating from Port Moresby,
New Guinea? 82

Why did Britain award the George Cross to the Island of Malta? 83

What was the Leigh Light? 83

How did Airey Neave manage to escape from a prisoner of war camp? 84

Which general turned the US II Corps into a tough fighting force? 84

What were the Baedeker Raids? 84

Which ship surprised the Japanese at the Battle of Midway? 85

When did the Americans fight against the French in the war? 85

How did a man survive for 133 days on a raft after his ship was sunk
by the Germans? 86

Which movie star did Hitler offer a reward for if captured? 86

Which soldier subdued three tanks with only a pistol? 86

How did a ship survive war with the Japanese by being disguised
as a tropical island? 87

Where were the first German POWs captured by Americans? 87

How many German POWs were held in the US? 87

How did five brothers change military policy about siblings
serving together? 88

1943 89

What was the smelliest escape ever attempted during World War II? 90

How was President Roosevelt almost killed by a torpedo? 90

Which army private had a song named after him for his bravery
in the South Pacific? 90

Where did the Americans first invade Europe? 91

Which British soldier smuggled himself in and out of Auschwitz? 91

How were hedgehogs and mousetraps used in the Battle of
the Atlantic? 92

What was the largest Jewish uprising during the war? 93

What change made to German U-boats in 1943 allowed them to stay
submerged for longer periods of time? 93

Why was a wagon full of cats the first vehicle brought into Leningrad when the blockade was broken? 94

Which German general surrendered the day after his promotion? 94

What happened to the Japanese man who planned the attack on Pearl Harbor? 94

What was Black May? 95

How did Mussolini escape after being deposed? 95

How were flares used in the Battle of the Ruhr? 96

What were bouncing bombs? 97

How did Britain create a firestorm to take out Hamburg? 97

What was the *la bataille du rail* (the Battle of the Rails)? 97

Who were the Chindits? 98

How did an American pilot take down a Japanese plane with a pistol? 98

What problem did the Americans face as they tried to land at Tarawa? 99

What unusual request did US General Dwight Eisenhower make in 1943? 100

What was the smallest army that fought in World War II? 100

Which US ship was actually a British ship? 101

Which German pilot escorted a wounded American pilot to safety? 101

How did an American ship take down a Japanese sub using potatoes? ... 102

How did an American convince 1,500 Japanese to surrender? 103

What role did Dr. Seuss play in the war? 103

1944 105

What musical instrument was played on the beach during the invasion of Normandy? 106

How did stealth mules help win the war? 106

What was the first ship sunk by a kamikaze pilot? 107

Which Black nurse defied orders and treated white soldiers? 108

Who were the Aztec Eagles? 108

What was the Lost Battalion? 109

How was the USS *Tang* sunk? 109

What was a pillbox and how did one play a role in the taking of
Cherbourg? 110

What was the only country in South America to fight in World War II? 110

Did German and American soldiers ever celebrate Christmas
together during the war? 111

Which Black Panther defied orders and continued to fight despite
a serious wound? 111

How did a silver dollar save a future senator's life? 112

How did a female war correspondent get to the front lines for D-Day? 113

What were strongholds and why did Hitler order them? 113

Why where there no marines on the beach at D-Day? 114

What type of boat was key to the Americans landing on D-Day? 114

What machine helped the Allied forces choose the best time for
D-Day? 115

What was the Red Ball Express? 116

How did an assassination attempt on Hitler's life almost end the war? . . . 116

What was Big Week? 117

What was the American response when the Germans demanded
they surrender at Bastogne? 117

What was the British Fourth Army? 118

How many Allied troops died on D-Day? 118

Which countries stormed which beaches at Normandy? 118

What was the name of the Allied operation for D-Day? 118

What happened at Bloody Nose Ridge? 119

Who were the first Black American troops to participate in combat
in the war? 119

Who was the highest-ranking American killed in the war? 119

Which relative of Hitler convinced the US president to let him serve
in the navy? 120

How did a Korean man end up being captured at Normandy on D-Day? . . . 120

Which soldier refused to accept a Distinguished Conduct Medal? 120

Which airman flew his plane underneath the Eiffel Tower? 121

Which spy received both British and German medals? 121

What was the American Ghost Army? 122

Who saved Paris from total destruction by the Nazis?.................122

What were paradummies?......................................123

Which rocket launched during the war was the first object to
reach space?..123

Who received a Bronze Star for a prayer? 123

1945......................................125

What was the name of the plane that dropped the atomic bomb
on Nagasaki, Japan?...126

Which American fought off over 100 Japanese soldiers?..............126

How did a toilet lead to the capture of a U-boat crew? 126

Which country used the largest battalion of flamethrower tanks
in the war? 127

What did American naval ships fly to celebrate the end of the war?......128

Which hospital ship was hit by a kamikaze attack? 128

How did the USO celebrate VJ Day?..............................128

Which ship did the Japanese formally surrender on? 129

How did the US Navy use a typhoon to help them take out
Japanese ships? 129

For which battle were the most Medals of Honor issued? 130

Which German general tried to surrender and then committed suicide?...130

How did a leper help the Americans win the Battle of Manila? 130

Which brand of pen was used by both General Eisenhower and
General MacArthur at VJ Day and VE Day surrender ceremonies? 131

How did a treacle factory stop a British tank? 131

What was the Prague uprising?.................................131

Which American war correspondent was killed on the field?...........132

How was napalm used in the invasion of Okinawa? 132

What happened to German U-boats at the end of the war?.............133

Which American president and commander in chief died in office
shortly before the end of the war?...............................133

Which Rhine bridge miraculously survived detonation attempts
by the Germans?...133

How were four American pilots killed after the war had ended? 134

Which battleship was sent on a suicide mission?.....................135

Which Japanese plot was kept quiet by the American news media?......135

How many bombs were dropped during the Battle of Dresden?..........135

Which battle from World War II made the *Guinness Book of World Records?*...136

What did General Patton do when he crossed the Rhine River in France for the first time?...136

Who brought down a German observation plane using only pistols?......136

Some Japanese survived the atom bombs at Nagasaki and Hiroshima, but did anyone survive both?.....................................137

Which American soldier saved 75 lives without ever touching a weapon?..137

Did the Germans and Americans ever fight on the same side in the war?...138

Why did a general order that a flag raised by troops be taken down during the Battle of Okinawa?......................................139

Who was the youngest marine to receive the Medal of Honor?..........139

When did the only submarine vs. submarine battle take place?.........140

After Germany surrendered, how did the US military decide which soldiers were sent to the Pacific?................................140

What new kind of submarine did the Japanese invent but never fully use?..141

How did a submarine take down a train?..........................141

What was the worst shark attack in history?.......................141

Which pilot took another plane down using just his propeller?..........142

REFERENCES 143

PHOTO CREDITS 144

ABOUT THE AUTHOR 146

INTRODUCTION

World War II is the deadliest war in the history of humankind. This war was fought on land, on sea, in the sky, in the desert, on mountains, in swamps, and in cities. Thirty countries were involved in the war, truly making it a world war. Seventy million people across the world served in the military in that war, and more than 60 million people died in the war. More than 6 million of those were Jewish people who were specifically targeted, captured, tortured, and killed by the Germans. During the war, these Jewish people were sent to concentration camps or death camps. This tragedy was known as "the Holocaust." The Holocaust is an incredibly important part of the war, but because this was not a battle, it is not specifically covered in this book. There are lots of great books to read about the Holocaust, and I encourage you to learn more about it.

Because American women and women in many countries were not permitted to enlist in the military, most of the facts in this book are about men. However, American women played very important roles in the war by working in factories and taking over the jobs soldiers left behind. They also did vital work as nurses and served in organizations such as the Red Cross and the USO (United Service Organizations). Most of the men who fought in the war were white. All of the American men in leadership positions during the war were also white. Although people of color were often not given important roles in the military, the men of color who served in the war did important jobs. We could not have won World War II without them.

This book is packed with fascinating and cool facts about the battles of World War II. It also covers interesting information about weapons, strategies, and what life was like for soldiers. It tells amazing stories about the heroes of the war. This book is not a complete history of the war though. You'll learn cool trivia and neat facts, but you won't get a complete picture of the war.

To be able to put all of this trivia in context, it's important to understand the war in general. Here's a summary of what happened.

World War II had two groups of countries fighting each other. The Allies included Great Britain, France, the Soviet Union (what is today Russia), Australia, Canada, Norway, Poland, New Zealand, and others, and eventually, the United States. The Axis countries included Germany, Italy, Japan, Hungary, Romania, and Bulgaria. The war began in 1939 and ended in 1945.

Franklin D. Roosevelt was the president of the United States when the war began. He died in office before the end of the war and was replaced by Harry S. Truman. Winston Churchill was the prime minister of Great Britain during the war. Emperor Hirohito was the ruler of Japan. Benito Mussolini was the prime minister of Italy. Adolf Hitler was the German chancellor. Joseph Stalin was the premier of the Soviet Union.

The war began in Europe. Hitler and his Nazi party had a plan for world domination. Germany invaded Poland and this started the war. The Atlantic Ocean was the scene of many important battles. German U-boats (*Unterseeboot*, which is German for submarine) waged war against the Allied ships. German fighter planes bombed the European Allied countries from the air. Germany began taking over other countries. They took over half of France. Battles were fought across Europe and in northern Africa. Germany invaded the Soviet Union, and the Soviets then joined the Allied Forces. The United States had remained neutral until this point.

The United States entered the war in 1941 when Japan bombed the American naval station at Pearl Harbor in Hawaii. The US then declared war on Japan. Germany then declared war on the US. The US joined the Allies and fought not only Japan, but the other Axis forces in Europe. The war against Japan was fought in the Pacific Ocean and on the islands in that ocean. The turning point of the war in the Pacific was the Battle of Midway in 1942, when the Allied forces won against the Japanese.

In Europe, the Allied forces won the conflict in North Africa by 1943. The Allies then took Italy. Mussolini, the Italian dictator, was unseated. On June 6, 1944, the Allied forces began a massive invasion of Europe by landing troops on the beaches of Normandy, France. This is called "D-Day." The Germans used all their resources to fight on the Western Front. Because of this, the Soviet Union was able to win the territories of Eastern Europe. The Battle of the Bulge was another turning point, with the Allies victorious. Germany surrendered on May 8, 1945. Hitler committed suicide just before the surrender.

The Japanese had not yet surrendered though. The battles in the Pacific were fierce. The Americans decided to drop a nuclear weapon on Japan. The atom bomb was dropped on Hiroshima and Nagasaki in August 1945. Japan then surrendered and the war was officially over.

Atomic bomb, Nagasaki

Now that you know the general facts about the war, you can start to learn some of the neat trivia.

WWII TIMELINE

1939

September 1: Germany invades Poland, beginning World War II.

September 3: Britain and France declare war on Germany. The first ship is sunk in the war (the SS *Athenia*).

September 3: The Battle of the Atlantic begins.

November 30: Germany invades Finland.

1940

May 10: Germany invades France, Belgium, and the Netherlands beginning the Battle of France.

May 26: Evacuation begins of Allied troops from Dunkirk, France.

June 10: Italy declares war on France and Great Britain.

June 22: France surrenders to Germany.

July 10: The Battle of Britain begins.

1941

May 24: The British ship *Hood* is sunk by Germany's *Bismarck*.

May 27: The *Bismarck* is sunk.

June 22: Germany invades the Soviet Union (Operation Barbarossa).

September 8: Siege of Leningrad begins.

September 30: The Battle of Moscow begins.

December 7: The Japanese attack Pearl Harbor, Hawaii, and declare war on the United States.

December 8: The United States declares war on Japan.

December 11: Germany and Italy declare war on the United States and the United States declares war on Germany and Italy.

1942

April 18: The Doolittle Raids on Tokyo occur.

May 12: The Second Battle of Kharkov begins.

June 4: The Battle of Midway begins.

July 1: The First Battle of El Alamein begins.

August 2: The Guadalcanal Campaign begins.

August 21: The Battle of Stalingrad begins.

October 23: The Second Battle of El Alamein begins.

November 8: The Allies invade North Africa (Operation Torch).

1943

February 2: The Germans surrender at Stalingrad in the Soviet Union.

April 19: The Warsaw Ghetto Uprising begins.

July 5: The Battle of Kursk begins.

July 25: Mussolini is deposed.

September 3: Italy surrenders.

1944

January 27: The Siege of Leningrad ends.

June 6: The D-Day invasion occurs, beginning the Battle of Normandy.

June 19: The Battle of the Philippine Sea occurs.

July 20: An assassination attempt against Hitler fails.

August 25: The Allies liberate Paris.

October 23: The Battle of Leyte Gulf begins.

December 16: The Battle of the Bulge begins.

1945

February 13: The Allies begin bombing Dresden.

February 19: The Battle of Iwo Jima begins.

April 1: The Battle of Okinawa occurs.

April 16: Battle of Berlin begins.

April 28: Mussolini is killed.

April 30: Adolf Hitler commits suicide.

May 7: Germany surrenders.

August 6: The United States drops the atomic bomb on Hiroshima, Japan.

August 9: The United States drops a second atomic bomb on Nagasaki, Japan.

August 15: Japan surrenders.

BATTLEFIELD LIFE

There were more than 70 million military members around the world who fought in World War II. These men fought on foot, in tanks, on ships, in planes, in submarines, in amphibious vehicles, and in trucks. They used all kinds of weapons, from knives and guns to anti-aircraft guns to bombs and nuclear weapons. Some of these men enlisted on their own. Others were drafted. Some wanted to fight. Others did not. This chapter shares little-known facts about the people and weapons that were involved in the war.

Q: How young was the youngest American to fight in the war?

A: Calvin Leon Graham was just 12 years old and in seventh grade when he enlisted (signed up for duty) to serve in the American navy. No one younger than 17 was allowed to enlist without a parent's consent. Calvin forged the consent and said he was 17. He tried to make his voice sound deeper, and he wore his older brother's clothes to try to look older. He served on the USS *South Dakota* and fought in the Battle of Guadalcanal. He was shot in the mouth and lost several teeth. Graham was given a Bronze Star for his bravery, even though he wasn't supposed to be fighting.

Q: What did battlefield soldiers use for toilet paper?

American soldiers each had 21 sheets of toilet paper per day. The German soldiers got three. If they ran out, they had to use leaves or pages from books they hid in their helmets or pockets.

Q: Why did Japanese soldiers wear special belts as part of their uniform?

A: The Japanese wore belts called *senninbari*. They were made of white cloth with 1,000 red stitches. The Japanese believed these belts brought them good luck and protected them from bullets. Their uniforms were olive green and the pants were usually short and wrapped tight at the knees.

Q: What was the standard-issue rifle used by the German infantry in World War II?

A: The Karabiner 98k was adopted by the Germans in 1935 and used throughout the war by the German infantry. It had bolt action and could hold five cartridges at a time. Each rifle came with a cleaning rod attached. A bayonet could be attached to the end.

Q: Which country lost the most people in World War II?

A: The Soviet Union lost the most people in the war. It is estimated that over 16 million Soviet citizens died in the war. Eighty percent of men born in that country in 1923 are believed to have died in the war.

Q: How much weight did the average US soldier carry in battle?

A: US soldiers carried gear that weighed 60 to 75 pounds. Their pack included socks, first aid items, food rations, a bayonet, canteen and mess kit, shovel for digging trenches, helmet, and a tent. Because the pack was so heavy, many wounded men drowned when they landed in Normandy during D-Day. They could not stay afloat and get from the boat to the shore with such a heavy load while injured.

American soldiers on their way to the front

Q: What was one of the most common injuries in the war that had nothing to do with bullets or bombs?

A: Trench foot was a common and very dangerous injury. Soldiers or sailors whose feet were wet for long periods of time developed trench foot. This could happen from constantly wearing wet socks and boots or from having their feet in water such as a swamp, a wet trench, or a leaking boat for days on end. If their feet were always wet, the skin would become infected with a fungus. The skin and then the nerves and blood vessels would be damaged. The feet could turn red, blister, peel, and the tissue could die. This was a serious problem that sent many soldiers to the hospital. Most never returned to battle because their injuries were so serious. Some of them had to have their feet amputated. Some even died from it.

Q: What battle cry did the Soviet soldiers often shout on the battlefield?

A: They shouted "*Ura!*" This means "kill."

Q: Which Japanese soldier remained at war the longest?

A: Hiroo Onoda was in the Japanese army when he was sent to Lubang Island with some other soldiers. The Japanese government ordered them to defend it against the Allies and not to surrender or commit suicide. In 1945, the Japanese on Lubang surrendered to the Allies. Onoda and three other soldiers escaped into the mountains. The Allies dropped leaflets on them to let them know the war was over. They thought it was a trap. Then the Japanese army dropped a leaflet ordering them to surrender. Onoda refused. In 1974 Onoda was found. He insisted he would not surrender unless a Japanese officer ordered him to. An officer in Japan then sent him the order and he finally surrendered. Onoda had remained at war for 29 years.

A: American soldiers who were fighting in the war often had to carry their own food with them. Because they were in dangerous situations, they didn't have cooks and mess halls to feed them. Soldiers were given crates of food to take with them into battle. There were two types of rations. C rations ("C" for combat) were the most commonly used rations. K rations were smaller, lighter meals given to paratroopers and airborne troops, which could fit in a pocket.

C rations were shipped in a box. Each box was supposed to have three meals and 3,600 calories. Inside the box were cans of pre-cooked food. The food could be eaten cold or heated up. The soldier had to use a tool called a key to open the can. The cans included things like hot dogs and beans, stew, eggs and ham, meat and hash, meat and noodles, or Spam. The box also had candy, chocolate, gum, salt, cheese spread, crackers, cigarettes, matches, toilet paper, and a wooden spoon. Later in the war, soldiers were also given powdered drinks to mix with water.

Some of the packages had paper labels on them and they often fell off, so soldiers didn't know what they were eating until they opened the food. Soldiers complained about the food and thought it tasted bad. In 1945, the US produced 105 million C rations.

Several foods we eat today were developed just for C rations including packaged sliced bread, Cheetos, Pringles, M&M's, instant coffee, and Chef Boyardee meals.

Q: For American sailors on ships in the Atlantic, what did the order "general quarters" mean?

A: When sailors were ordered to their general quarters, it meant that they were required to all go to their individual battle stations. Every single weapon, sensor, and firefighting station would be manned, and the captain of the ship would be on the bridge. Everyone was on watch for U-boats and ready to fight to protect their ship.

Q: How many U-boats did the Germans use during World War II?

A: At the end of World War I, Germany was forbidden from building U-boats. By 1935, Germany renegotiated the treaty terms and began building U-boats. During World War II, Germany built 1,162 U-boats. Seven hundred eighty-five were destroyed in the war. The rest surrendered or were scuttled (sunk by their crew).

Q: What luxury did American submarines have?

A: Life on submarines was hard. Sailors had to live in tiny, cramped spaces. Each had one bunk to himself. The rest of the space was crammed with equipment and weapons. Food was stowed every-where possible, including in the showers and under the bunks. Because things were so crowded and uncomfortable, the Navy made sure the submarine sailors had good food. One special luxury on each ship was an ice cream freezer, so the crew could have ice cream to enjoy.

Q: What was the Momsen lung?

A: The Momsen lung was a piece of lifesaving equipment used on American submarines. It was made of a rubber bag with two tubes. One tube was for inhaling and one was for exhaling. The air would go into the bag, which had soda lime in it. This removed carbon dioxide from the air. Sailors could strap on a Momsen lung when they escaped from a sunken submarine and use it to breathe until they could get to the surface. It also helped them rise slowly so they didn't get the bends (this is a kind of sickness that happens from coming up from deep water too quickly).

Training recruits to use the Momsen lung

Q: Why did the air in submarines smell so bad during the war?

A: Submarines were very small with a limited amount of air. The subs stayed submerged during daylight and only surfaced at night. This meant that the subs were underwater with no fresh air for up to 16 hours a day. The engines heated up the air, bringing the temperature in the engine room up to 100°F. Mold grew inside the subs. Up to 80 men worked in the small, hot spaces of the sub and they sweated. There was limited fresh water available so most men only showered once every 10 days. There wasn't enough water to do laundry. As you can imagine, all of this meant it smelled pretty bad inside.

Q: What was the most popular dish at the Honolulu USO?

A: The USO (United Service Organizations) was devoted to helping to boost the troops' morale during the war. They had over 3,000 clubs worldwide during the war where American servicemen could come to hear music, dance, and eat. The USO raised $33 million during the war to provide entertainment and comfort to troops. They often hosted big-name entertainers who flew all over the world to perform for the troops (one of the most famous was an entertainer named Bob Hope). Men often spent time at the USO clubs when they were on leave from the battlefront. The club in Honolulu was famous for its banana splits. At the height of the war, the club used one ton of bananas and 250 gallons of ice cream per day to feed the troops who visited.

Q: What luxury did US hospital ships have?

A: Hospital ships played an important role in the war, providing fast treatment for servicemen wounded or injured in battle. They were huge floating hospitals. The USS *Benevolence* could care for 802 patients and carried more than 500 medical professionals and staff.

USS *Benevolence*

The ships had special hoists for bringing patients onto the ship. They had labs and even special rooms for treating patients who were in shock. The *Benevolence* had four operating rooms, a psychiatric unit, a dental unit, and a physical therapy unit. These ships also brought along field hospitals in crates that could be set up on land near battle lines. They had an ambulance to go with the field hospital. The ships had more than just medical space. They had special areas for the men who were recuperating. There were lounges and a five-channel music system with earphones in each bed. The *Benevolence* and other ships like it also had air-conditioning, a rare luxury of the time.

Q: What was the largest cause of death in World War II?

A: More than 60 million people died due to World War II. Although 19.5 million people died fighting in the war, bombs and guns were not the biggest cause of death. More than 20 million people died of starvation during the war. Some starvation was intentional, such as the way the Germans treated the Jewish people they held in camps. Other starvation was unintentional but happened because food was short supply in many regions of the world. A million people alone died of starvation in the siege of Leningrad.

Q: How many deceased American soldiers' bodies were never returned home after the war?

A: Of the more than 400,000 American soldiers who died in the war, many were never brought home for burial. At the end of the war, 79,000 were classified as Missing in Action (MIA). Many bodies were recovered and buried, but not identified. The number of American World War II soldiers buried as unknown soldiers is more than 9,400. This does not include the numbers of soldiers and sailors who were lost at sea.

Q: How did Monopoly games help some soldiers escape?

A: Britain worked with the company that made Monopoly games to create special editions for British POWs held by the Axis forces.

The games included secret escape maps printed on silk, tiny tools, compasses, and real money mixed in with the Monopoly money to help the POWs escape. Each game had a special red dot on the Free Parking space to indicate it was a special edition. Specific editions were created for different parts of Europe, with maps just for those areas and currency for the country in question. The British created fake charity groups who delivered the games to the German POW camps. The soldiers were told about the games as part of their training so they would know how to spot them.

Q: What was a battlefield cross?

A: When a soldier was killed in battle, it was common for his fellow soldiers to create a small memorial where he died. The soldier's rifle with bayonet attached would be placed bayonet down into the ground, with the rifle stock standing up. The soldier's boots would be placed on either side of the rifle. The soldier's dog tags would be hung on the rifle. The helmet would be placed on the rifle stock.

Q: Who was named a Crow Tribe war chief for his acts during the war?

A: Jim Medicine Crow was a member of the Crow Tribe. He enlisted in 1943. He wore war paint underneath his uniform. While he served, he completed the four acts of bravery required to become a war chief of his tribe:

- He helped lead war parties behind enemy lines.
- He stole enemy horses.
- He disarmed a member of the enemy.
- He fought in hand-to-hand combat with an enemy and overcame him without killing him.

When he returned from the war he was named as a war chief. He also received the Presidential Medal of Freedom.

Q: What were banzai attacks?

A: Banzai attacks were a method used by the Japanese soldiers in the battles in the Pacific theater. A group of Japanese soldiers would simply run at the enemy with their bayonets out. The goal was to kill as many as they could before they were killed. It was considered a type of suicide mission. Near the end of the war these attacks were almost never successful since the Allied troops fought back with machine guns and semi-automatic rifles. This method was often used as a last-ditch effort.

Q: What was it like when a battleship fired at the enemy?

A: When a battleship fired, the entire ship was affected. Hundreds of pounds of gunpowder exploded with each shot. The force of the explosion could cause toilets to crack and sailors' bones to break. The deck could start on fire and needed to be swabbed between each shot. The air would fill with smoke, making it hard to breathe or see.

Q: Which country suffered the highest percentage loss of its population in the war?

A: By the end of the war, one-fifth of the population of Poland had died. The losses happened in battles, from starvation, and from purposeful extermination by the Germans and Soviets. This was the highest percentage loss of life in the war.

Q: How many naval mines were laid during the war?

A: A naval mine is an explosive device placed in the water. It is set off when a ship comes near it or touches it. About half a million mines were laid during World War II by all the nations involved.

Q: How much were American soldiers paid during the war?

A: A private in the US army was paid $50 a month, which is about $740 in today's dollars.

Q: What was an elephant gun?

A: The Lahti L-39 20 mm anti-tank rifle was used by the Finnish forces against the Soviet Union. It had a ski mounting so that it could be used on snow. It had a 10-round magazine and a cheek rest.

**Q: What was *Englandspiel?*

A: The British placed intelligence officers in the Netherlands. These officers used radios to send important information back to Britain, and Britain shared information with them about their wartime plans. The intelligence officers had secret code words they were supposed to use in their messages if they had been captured. From 1942 to 1944, several British intelligence officers were captured by the Germans. The Germans forced them to send false updates back to Britain. The agents included the secret code words, but they were ignored by the British. The British kept sending new information to the captured agents. This allowed the Germans to have advance notice of operations the British planned. The British kept sending new secret agents into the Netherlands by parachute. The Germans would be waiting for them and would capture them. Because they got the spies' messages, the Germans also knew where British planes were going to land. They would allow the landing but then shoot the planes when they took off for Britain. Twelve British air force (called the Royal Air Force or RAF) planes were lost due to this strategy. The Germans called this situation *Englandspiel* (which means "England game" in German).

Q: What was the Flying Fortress?

A: The American B-17 bomber plane was called "the Flying Fortress." It had 10 machine guns and four gunners. When it was introduced it had more power than any British or German plane. It was used in daylight bombing raids against Germany. This type of plane dropped more bombs than any other during the war.

B-17 Bomber over Germany

Q: What was a Little Katie?

A: A Little Katie was the Soviet Katyusha rocket on a launcher. This rocket was launched from a truck and could be easily moved around. This made them challenging to fight against. However, they were not very accurate and were time-consuming to reload.

Q: What was a human torpedo?

A: A human torpedo was a manned torpedo first used by the Italians. Two riders would steer the torpedo through the water with a propeller. When they got close to a ship, they would attach it to the ship with a timer. The drivers would get away and the bomb would go off soon after. The British soon created their own human torpedo and called it "the Chariot."

Q: How did decks of cards help American POWs?

A: The Bicycle playing card company created a special deck of cards for American soldiers during the war. It was called a "Map Deck." When the cards were soaked in water, they would peel apart to show maps hidden inside them. The maps showed secret escape routes the soldiers could use if they escaped from POW camps.

Q: Who were the Seabees?

A: After the United States entered the war, the naval command realized they needed people to build bases and camps overseas. The navy formed the Seabees, a group of civilian engineers. The Seabees would be sent in once an area was secured. They would unload supplies and start creating roads, airstrips, hospitals, and buildings. Their motto was "We Build, They Fight." The Seabees built over 400 advanced bases throughout the war.

Q: What was the doodlebug?

A: The doodlebug or buzz bomb was the German V-1 bomb, which was a flying bomb. Each one had wings and a jet engine. They made a buzzing noise when they flew. They flew in a straight and level line and were somewhat easy to shoot down. Despite this,

33,000 people were killed in Britain by this bomb and another similar version.

Q: How many prisoners of war were taken during World War II?

A: There were about 14 million prisoners of war taken throughout the war (9 million by Axis forces and 5 million by Allied forces). This was the largest number of POWs involved in any war.

Polish POWs after a German invasion

Q: How much did the war cost?

A: It is estimated that the cost to all the countries involved was more than 1 trillion dollars. In today's dollars, that is 14.46 trillion dollars.

Q: What was in British RAF crews' survival kits?

A: British RAF aircrews had to be prepared in case they needed to parachute out of their planes. They were given survival kits that included candy, a compass, and water purification tablets.

Q: What special footwear was issued to US airborne troops?

A: United States airborne troops were all given special boots called "jump boots." These special boots had extra ankle support so that when the men landed from their parachutes they wouldn't twist their ankles.

Q: What was the Baka?

A: The Baka ("idiot bomb") was the name American soldiers gave to a type of Japanese bomb. The Japanese called this bomb *Ohka* ("cherry blossom"). The bomb was dropped by a plane. A pilot rode inside the bomb, which had wings and an engine. Once it was dropped, it would glide through the air until the pilot saw the target. He would turn the engine on and the bomb would fly quickly towards the target. The bomb was easy to target after launch, but hard to stop once its engine was turned on. The pilot died when the bomb exploded.

Q: What did American troops read while on the battlefield?

A: In between battles, troops had a lot of downtime and needed things to do. Libraries held book drives (called "the Victory Book Campaign") to get books to send to troops, but this often resulted in troops getting books they were not interested in. Hardcover books were difficult for soldiers to carry with them. Publishers began to print small paperback novels that used lightweight newsprint for pages. In all, 120 million books were produced. The Armed Services Editions (ASE) were free for soldiers. The books were designed to fit in a soldier's breast pocket. Each book was supposed to last through six readings, but soldiers often used them for longer.

All kinds of books including Shakespeare, westerns, and mysteries were printed. Romances were also in high demand. One of the most popular books was *A Tree Grows in Brooklyn* by Betty Smith because it made them think about home. Another popular title was *Chicken Every Sunday* by Rosemary Taylor. This book was about a boarding house and described the dinners served there. For soldiers who were eating C rations, the descriptions of the food made them happy. F. Scott Fitzgerald's book *The Great Gatsby* did not do well when it was originally published. But after it was issued as an ASE book, it became popular and now is considered a classic. Soldiers often wrote fan letters to the authors of the books.

The books helped to boost soldiers' morale. They would pass them around and some read them aloud so they could all enjoy them. The publishing and distribution of these books countered Hitler's book burnings. The Nazis burned over 100 million books, but this program put more books into the world than the Nazis could burn. Before the war, few publishers printed paperbacks, but the ASE program resulted in the first mass production of paperbacks. Paperbacks became standard after the war.

After the war, many soldiers went to college on the GI Bill (a law that let them go to college for free). The free books program is credited with keeping the troops interested in reading, and many soldiers said the program is what made them interested in going to college after the war.

Q: What were Foo Fighters?

A: At various points in the war in Europe, American airmen would see strange lights in the sky. The lights would rise up into the sky, seem to follow their planes, and just disappear. The lights were often orange or red. The airmen started calling these mysterious lights Foo Fighters. At the time there was a comic strip about a fire-fighter called "Smokey Stover." He often said, "Where there's foo, there's fire." That's where the name came from. Later the name was used by an American rock band. An Army Air Command team was sent to investigate but the report they wrote was lost after the war. Other investigations never determined what actually caused these sightings.

Q: What were Jericho Trumpets?

A: German Stuka dive-bombers had sirens on their wings called "Jericho Trumpets." The idea was that the sound of the sirens would create fear in the area the planes flew over. This was true, but it also soon served as an early warning. The sirens created drag and slowed the planes down though, so they were eventually discontinued.

Q: What were the Para Dogs?

A: British paratroopers had German shepherds who parachuted with them out of planes. The dogs were used to sniff out mines and to act as guards.

Q: What was one of the biggest dangers facing pilots in the war?

A: Although getting shot at was a major concern, pilots faced serious injury from frostbite on many flights. Pilots of B-17s and B-24s flew in planes that were not pressurized or heated. They flew at altitudes of over 2,500 feet and encountered temperatures between -30°F and -50°F. Frostbite was a constant problem.

Q: What was the standard issue field coat for US soldiers in the war?

A: The US M1941 field jacket was issued to every American soldier in the war. The coat was specially designed for the war. It replaced a wool coat that could only be dry-cleaned. The field jacket was named after Major General J. K. Parsons who was in charge of designing it. The jacket was designed by the army and sent to *Esquire* (a men's fashion magazine) to be reviewed. The staff at the magazine recommended many improvements but the army ignored them all. Soldiers had a lot of problems with the jacket. It didn't keep soldiers warm and didn't protect them from wind or rain. It was made in a beige color that was supposed to be helpful in camouflaging soldiers, but the color faded. Many soldiers wore it inside out once this happened. It didn't have big pockets.

Q: How many German generals died in the war?

A: Two hundred and nineteen German generals were killed in the war. Of those, 135 died in combat and 84 were executed by Hitler.

Q: How many American generals died in the war?

A: Only 40 American generals died during or immediately after the war. Eleven were killed in action. Two were killed while being held as POWs. Four died in plane crashes. One died as a result of friendly fire. The rest died from natural causes.

Q: How did a Hungarian mathematician save the lives of many American air force men?

A: During the war, the American military was considering how best to cover their planes in armor to prevent them from being shot down. They studied all the planes that had been shot yet made it back. They were going to put armor on new planes in the areas where those planes had the most damage. Hungarian mathematician Abraham Wald looked at the plans and realized the military had "survivor bias." They were looking only at the planes that had been shot and made it back. They were not considering the planes that had been shot down, which never came home to be studied. Those planes were likely shot in other places. Wald estimated where those downed planes had been hit most often and helped the military plan to armor new planes in those areas. If he hadn't helped, new planes would only have been armored in places where they had been shot yet survived. The new planes would not have had armor in the most vulnerable areas, which caused them to crash when shot.

Q: Why did some troops eat steak and eggs for breakfast?

A: It was routine for troops that were going to do an amphibious landing to eat steak and eggs for breakfast the morning of the attack. The thinking was it would give them energy. It was good for morale and gave the troops something to look forward to before putting their lives at risk. Unfortunately, it actually ended up endangering them. Reports showed that having that in their stomachs actually made abdominal wounds more dangerous.

Q: How did a bear travel with Polish troops during the war?

A: Wojtek the bear was found by the 22nd Transport Company's Artillery Division in the Polish II Corps in Iran and adopted by them. He traveled with them wherever they went, including to Italy. They fed him condensed milk and beer. He also ate cigarettes. He would chase oranges the men threw as practice grenades. In the Battle of Monte Cassino he was seen unloading crates and empty shells. After this, the regiment changed their insignia (badge) to that of a bear carrying a shell.

Q: What was unique about US General MacArthur's hat?

A: US General Douglas MacArthur did not wear a regulation-issued hat during the war. MacArthur spent time before the war in the Philippines and actually retired from the army while there. The Filipino president hired him as a military advisor and named him as a field marshal of the Philippine army. MacArthur designed his own hat for the role. When World War II began, MacArthur rejoined the US army and continued to wear the hat. MacArthur is also famous for the corncob pipe he often had in his mouth. He designed that himself as well.

MacArthur in his special hat and corncob pipe

Q: How did matchbooks impact the German army?

A: Allied forces dropped matchbooks over German forces in Europe. The matchbooks had instructions for how to fake an illness so the German soldiers could be sent home. Some soldiers followed this advice. However, the commanders soon learned about this and then refused to believe those who claimed to be sick. This meant soldiers who were actually ill had to fight, and likely could not fight well while ill.

Q: **How many men who served in the war later became president of the United States?**

A: Seven men who served were later elected president. The following American presidents served in World War II:

- Dwight D. Eisenhower
- John F. Kennedy
- Lyndon B. Johnson
- Richard M. Nixon
- Gerald R. Ford
- Ronald Reagan
- George H. W. Bush

1939

The world went to war for the second time in 1939. World War II officially started on September 1, 1939, when Germany invaded Poland. Before this though, Hitler was planning the invasion. He signed a secret pact with the Soviet Union that they would share Poland. Two days after Germany invaded Poland, Britain and France declared war against Germany. The United States decided to stay neutral and not get involved in the war. Then the Soviet Union invaded Poland and won the Battle of Warsaw. Soon after, the Soviet Union invaded Finland. Hitler was determined to take over much of Europe.

Q: What was the first battle of World War II?

A: There are several possible answers to this question. The first conflict of World War II could be considered to have been on September 1, 1939, when Germany invaded Poland. The first actual battle could be considered the Battle of the Bzura, when Polish troops fought against German troops on September 9, 1939.

Polish cavalry in the Battle of the Bzura

Q: How did math result in the scuttle of a German ship?

A: On December 13, 1939, the German battleship *Graf Spee* was sinking British supply ships in the South Atlantic. The British sent four cruiser ships in response. Commodore Henry Harwood was in charge of the HMS *Ajax*, HMS *Exeter*, HMS *Cumberland*, and HMS *Achilles*. Harwood found out the Germans had sunk two ships in the area.

Harwood used math to figure out where the German ship would move so he could attack it. He calculated the distance between the two supply ships the Germans sank and found out the times each was sunk. From that he knew how fast the German ship was traveling. He used that to figure out how far the ship would have traveled since it last attacked. He sent his ships to the mouth of the River Plate in Argentina, calculating that the German ship would be there next. He was right.

Graf Spee came to the river and saw the masts of the British ships from far away. She changed her engines into battle mode, which sent up a big puff of black smoke into the sky. The British saw it and knew right where she was. The ships fought with torpedoes and guns. The *Graf Spee* was so damaged she

Graf Spee, scuttled

gave up and pulled into the harbor in Uruguay, which was a neutral country. The Germans scuttled the ship (sank it themselves). The battle was over and the Allied forces won.

Q: Which wartime strategy memo was likely influenced by a famous author?

A: Ian Fleming, the creator of the popular James Bond character, served in British Naval Intelligence as assistant to Rear Admiral John Godfrey. Fleming's books (which were made into the famous James Bond movies) often included clever operations. It's believed that even when he was in the military, Fleming was coming up with these kinds of ideas. In 1939 when Fleming worked for Godfrey, Godfrey issued the Trout Memo, a document with lots of secret strategy ideas. One idea was to put fake information on a corpse dressed up as a member of the British military and float it into the Germans. The plan was the Germans would think the planted information was true and be fooled. This ended up being used and was called "Operation Mincemeat."

Q: Who fought on skis in the war?

A: Finnish ski troops fought on cross-country skis. The Soviet Union invaded Finland on November 30, 1939, after an attempt to negotiate for more territory. The Finns fought back from trenches and bunkers. Although this is generally considered part of World War II, it is called "the Winter War." Eleven ski battalions fought against the Soviets by moving among the trees in the forests. Because they wore white uniforms to blend in with the snow (the Soviets' green uniforms stuck out), they were called "Ghost Soldiers." They threw Molotov cocktails (bottles filled with flammable material that bursts into flame when thrown) into tanks, blowing them up. Eventually the Soviets proved stronger and Finland signed a treaty in 1940, giving in to them.

Finnish ski patrols

Q: What was the first ship sunk in World War II?

A: The first ship sunk in the war was not a battleship. It was the British ship SS *Athenia*, a transatlantic passenger ship. A German U-boat sunk her with a torpedo on September 3, 1939, just hours after Britain declared war on Germany. More than 1,000 passengers were on board (including 300 Americans). Of them, 117 died. It took 14 hours for the ship to sink.

Q: What was the Phony War?

A: In September 1939, The Germans invaded Poland. Britain, and France, and then declared war on Germany. And then nothing happened for six months. The Germans couldn't decide what to do next and just spent the time training their troops. The Allies put a naval blockade in place to keep Germany from getting needed supplies. There was no actual fighting during this period of time, so it was called "the Phony War."

Q: Why did Germany attack Poland and start the war?

A: Germany was seeking to take back territory it believed it was entitled to and to expand its rule. Germany claimed that Poland had been plotting with Britain and French to surround Germany and take away its power. Germany also claimed that the Polish people had been persecuting Germans who

German troops marching in Warsaw, Poland

lived there. The military, along with the SS (the military arm of the Nazi party) even staged a fake attack by Poland against Germany and broadcast it on German radio. Germany then used this "attack" as the reason to invade Poland.

Q: Why did Britain order a million coffins in preparation for the war?

A: Once Germany invaded Poland, Britain began preparing for war. A major concern was the safety of citizens in London. The German Luftwaffe (air force) was strong and Britain knew that it would bomb London. The British military feared there would be many casualties. In fact, they predicted up to a million people could die in the bombings, so they ordered a million caskets to be prepared. Ultimately, more than 450,000 British civilians and military members died in the war.

Q: Although the United States remained neutral when the war began in 1939, what did the president urge Americans to do?

A: On September 3, 1939, Britain and France went to war with Germany. US President Franklin D. Roosevelt declared the United States as neutral. However, he said, "This nation will remain a neutral nation, but I cannot ask that every American remain neutral in thought as well. Even a neutral has a right to take account of facts. Even a neutral cannot be asked to close his mind or his conscience."

Q: How many tanks did Germany send into Poland during the invasion?

A: Germany sent 2,500 tanks, 2,000 planes, and 1.5 million troops into Poland, significantly outnumbering the Polish military.

Q: Why did the Soviet Union invade Poland?

A: The Soviets had made a secret pact with Germany that allowed them to invade Poland. The Soviets claimed that their relations, the Ukrainians and Byelorussians, were trapped in an area that Poland had illegally taken. Their justification for the invasion was that they needed to rescue them.

Q: How successful was France at defending its ally Poland when it was invaded by the Germans?

A: The French efforts to aid Poland were minimal. The French pushed five miles into Poland and then retreated. They set up a defensive line at their own border and stayed there.

Q: How did Poland's military compare to Germany's?

A: When the Germans invaded Poland in 1939, Poland had 30 infantry divisions. Eleven of these were cavalry divisions and two were mechanized. The Germans had the strong Luftwaffe and 40 divisions of infantry, including six armored divisions and 10 mechanized divisions. Poland was no match for the German military.

Q: How much of a defense did Poland mount when the Soviet Union attacked?

A: The Soviet Union invaded Poland on September 17, 1939. This was part of their secret pact with Germany. When the Soviet troops crossed Poland's eastern border, there were no Polish forces there at all to fight. The Soviets were not challenged. Only 1,000 Soviet troops were killed in their entire occupation of eastern Poland.

Q: Why were the snakes in the London Zoo killed in 1939?

A: The snakes were killed because the British government was concerned a bomb dropped by Germany could result in them being set free. If the snakes were free, they could move around the city and hurt people.

Q: Why was Germany's invasion of Belgium and France postponed twice?

A: Germany planned to invade France and Belgium in November of 1939, but it had to be postponed due to bad weather. The invasion was rescheduled for January 1940 but was postponed again after the Allies learned of the date of the plan.

Q: What action did France take during the Phony War?

A: Although in general there was no activity during the Phony War (see page 33), France did march troops 16 miles inside Germany in September 1939. They quickly withdrew, though, and saw no action.

Q: How badly were Finnish forces outnumbered by Soviet forces?

A: The Soviets wanted Finland to trade them some land near Leningrad in exchange for a piece of unusable land in Karelia. Finland refused. The Soviets attacked at the Finnish border on November 20, 1939. The Soviets had half a million soldiers. Finland had 130,000. Despite being so badly outnumbered, the Finnish held out behind the Mannerheim Line, a system of fortifications. That, combined with the ski force (see page 32) and the wintery conditions the Soviets were not used to, allowed the Finnish to hold off the Soviets during 1939.

Q: How was the British battleship *Royal Oak* sunk?

A: The battleship HMS *Royal Oak* was anchored in Scapa Flow in the Orkney Islands in Scotland on October 13, 1939. This harbor was believed to be completely protected and not vulnerable to attack by the Germans. German U-boat *U-47* got into the harbor at night and sank the ship. It was the first battleship that was sunk in the war. Eight hundred and thirty-five sailors were killed. The ship remains upside down under the water where she was sunk.

HMS *Royal Oak*

Q: What was the Venlo Incident?

A: In November 1939, two British intelligence officers in the Netherlands were trying to make contact with anti-Nazi forces inside Germany. German troops captured the officers in the Dutch town of Venlo and took them to Germany where they were interrogated. The officers gave up important secret information, including the names of other intelligence officers who were working in Europe. Hitler used this incident as part of his basis for invading the Netherlands.

Q: What was the name of the ship that fired the first shots of the war?

A: The first shots of the war were fired from the German ship SMS *Schleswig-Holstein* on September 1, 1939. The Germans opened fire on a Polish fortress.

Q: How did Germany capture Czechoslovakia without any warfare?

A: Hitler met with the Czech president Emil Hácha on March 15, 1939. Hitler wanted possession of Czechoslovakia. Hácha refused. Hitler threated to bomb the capital, Prague. Hácha gave in and agreed Germany could use the country. The country became part of Germany without any battles.

Q: What was the Sausage War?

A: There's a saying: "An army marches on its stomach." The Sausage War proved this to be true. During the Winter War (see page 32), the Soviet Union invaded Finland. Soviet leaders did not expect Finland to fight outdoors in the winter. But the Finnish people were used to winter. The Soviets were unprepared for winter fighting conditions in Finland. The Soviet soldiers had only their summer uniforms. They were not trained to fight in winter conditions. Their food supplies were small. They had to survive on black bread and dried meat. The Soviet soldiers were hungry and cold.

The Soviet soldiers were not in good spirits. The Finns had just launched a nighttime sneak attack on a Soviet battalion. The Finns opened fire and then skied away. They then attacked another battalion and skied away. The two Soviet battalions ended up mistakenly fighting each other until they realized what happened.

On December 10, 1939, the Soviets attempted a sneak attack of their own at Ilomantsi in Finland. The Soviets advanced on the Finnish camp, ready to fight them. The Finns retreated (leaving their camp behind), and the Soviets were supposed to follow them. But then they smelled the sausage stew the Finns had been cooking in their tents. The Soviet soldiers were starving. They couldn't resist the smell of the sausage. They stopped to eat.

The Finns came back and attacked the Soviets. They fought in hand-to-hand combat, using bayonets, knives, tools, pistols, and submarine guns to kill the Soviets. Within minutes, all of the Soviets were killed or scattered in the woods. Some of them died with sausages in their mouths and stuffed in their pockets. Over 100 Soviets were killed.

The Finns were victorious that night. The episode shows that to be effective an army must be fed well. Hungry troops are easily distracted.

1940

The year 1940 was a difficult one for the Allied forces. Germany conquered Denmark, Norway, the Netherlands, Belgium, and France. They then moved on Britain. The long and difficult Battle of Britain raged throughout this year. Britain and Allied troops were forced to evacuate the city of Dunkirk in France. Italy created a pact with Hitler and entered the war, declaring war on France and Britain.

Q: How were balloons used to fight the war?

A: During the Battle of Britain in 1940, the British released thousands of huge 62-foot-long balloons into the sky above Britain. The balloons were filled with gas that was lighter than air and were tied to the ground by long chains. The Germans

British barrage balloon

were conducting air raids and bombing Britain. The balloons got in their way and forced them to fly higher to avoid the balloons and the cables they were attached to. This made their air raids less accurate. Fifteen thousand British women were trained to put up the balloons. They were part of the Women's Auxiliary Air Force in Britain.

Q: What was the shortest battle of World War II?

A: The Battle of Denmark on April 9, 1940, lasted just two hours. The Germans invaded Denmark. After two hours of fighting, the Danish prime minister pulled all the troops back. Six hours later, Danish King Christian X surrendered.

Q: What does "blitzkrieg" mean in German?

A: "Blitzkrieg" means "lightning war" in German. Blitzkrieg was the approach used by the Germans in the war starting in 1940. Instead of sending their forces to a lot of different places, they moved them in large groups, hitting specific targets hard. They used mobile forces, like planes and tanks, rather than soldiers on foot, fighting in trenches, as they did in World War I. When the Germans began bombing Britain from planes, it was referred to as "the blitz."

Q: How did old biplanes hold off the Italians?

A: When the war began, Malta, a small archipelago between Tunisia and Sicily, belonged to Britain. Its military post was an important one because of its location in the Mediterranean. Italy began attacking Malta by air in June 1940. Britain had almost no resources on Malta and no planes. They had little defense.

An air commodore in the RAF found some packing crates that had been left. Inside them were the pieces of Gladiator biplanes. This old-fashioned plane couldn't compete with the Italian air force, but it was all the British had. They put the planes together and got three of them in the air. They named them Faith, Hope, and Charity.

The planes flew above Malta, giving hope to the Maltese people as well as the British stationed there. The planes flew for ten days, engaging with the Italians. Sometimes the biplanes flew with a hundred Italian planes swarming around them. Despite the outdated nature of the planes, they shot down several Italian planes. The planes kept the Italians busy and confused, so that some of their bombs didn't hit their targets. The pilots' bravery kept the Italians at bay until more reinforcements could arrive.

Q: How did the United States supply Britain with planes despite a neutrality agreement?

A: The United States had several neutrality agreements in place in 1940. One of the agreements was that the US could not fly its planes into another country to aid in the war. Britain desperately needed planes and the US had them. To get around the rules, planes were flown to the US–Canada border and landed there. Then the Canadians towed them over the border and flew them to Britain to aid in the war. This way the US didn't fly the planes to another country and didn't violate the agreements.

Q: Which fighter plane was developed in just 102 days?

A: The North American P-51 Mustang was developed by North American Aviation when the British asked them to develop planes for the war. The prototype was created in 102 days and was ready on September 9, 1940. It flew just a few weeks later. It could fly at 400 miles per hour and could carry 1,000 pounds. It was outfitted with six .50-caliber M2 Browning machine guns. This aircraft helped turn the tide of the war. These planes took down almost 5,000 enemy planes in battle.

Pilots of the 15th Air Force in Italy in front of a P-51 Mustang.

Q: How did the Germans sneak into France to occupy it?

A: France was considered to have one of the strongest militaries in the world. The Maginot Line ran along the eastern front and was considered impenetrable. To the north, the British were prepared to keep the Germans from invading from Belgium. Hitler did what no one expected instead. He sent troops in through the northeast corner of France, through the Ardennes hills. The French believed the roads were impassable in that area, but Hitler proved them wrong.

Q: Who was the only soldier who killed with a longbow during the war?

A: British Reserve Officer "Fighting" Jack Churchill was sent to France in 1940. After the Battle of L'Epinette, Churchill and his team were trapped by Germans. Churchill used his longbow to kill a German soldier and got his company out of danger. In addition to the longbow, Churchill also carried a sword and often played the bagpipes for his troops. Churchill was not related to British Prime Minister Winston Churchill.

Q: Which vehicle was inspired by a hurricane?

A: The LVT (Landing Vehicle Tracked), or Alligator, was commissioned by the American military in 1940. Donald Roebling lived in Florida when the Okeechobee Hurricane came through. At least 2,500 people died. It was followed by several other hurricanes. Roebling went to work trying to invent an amphibious vehicle he could use to rescue people trapped by the hurricane floodwaters. The Army contracted him to build them in 1940. Each vehicle cost $24,000. They weighed 7,700 pounds each and could carry 7,000 pounds. They traveled at 4 miles per hour on water and 29 on land. The original model had a Chrysler engine, and the final version had an airplane engine. LVTs were used in many locations during the war, but most famously on Iwo Jima.

LVTs approach Iwo Jima

Q: **What were bomb cemeteries?**

A: London was regularly bombed by German aircraft during the Blitz, which lasted from September 1940 through May 1941. While many of the bombs caused incredible damage, others landed intact. Brave, highly skilled military members were sent to disarm the bombs. Once the bombs were disarmed, they were taken to bomb cemeteries, large open spaces, and detonated.

Q: **What was the Miracle at Dunkirk?**

A: In May of 1940, the Germans began the Blitzkrieg in Europe. The Germans occupied France and pushed the Allied troops to the sea at the French port of Dunkirk. The British needed to get their troops out. They launched Operation Dynamo. The port at Dunkirk was very shallow so the Royal Navy ships could not reach the shore.

Instead, many civilian boats were used to remove the troops. By the end of the evacuation, 338,000 British and French troops were taken to safety. This was called "the Miracle at Dunkirk."

Q: What was the cavity magnetron?

A: In 1940 at Birmingham University in England, two researchers invented the cavity magnetron. This small handheld device could send out pulses of microwave energy. This little piece of equipment improved radar technology, increasing the distance at which objects could be spotted. The technology not only helped win the war but changed the way we cook. One of the researchers was standing in front of one of the new radar machines that used the microwave technology and a candy bar in his pocket melted. He experimented with different kinds of food (including popcorn) with the microwaves. This led to the invention of the microwave oven.

Q: What popular vehicle was invented as America prepared for war?

A: In 1940, the United States had not yet entered the war but was preparing to do so. The Army needed a new military transport vehicle that could be used on all kinds of terrain. Three American companies built prototypes. Eventually all three companies began making the same type of vehicle, which was called a "Jeep."

Q: What strategy did the Germans use to gain a foothold in Norway?

A: Instead of sending in troops on foot, Germany used another strategy to hold positions in Norway in 1940. The Germans sent paratroopers in to secure strategic places such as airfields and bridges. This strategy proved highly effective.

Q: Where was the surrender ceremony held when France surrendered to Germany?

A: France surrendered to Germany on June 22, 1940. The ceremony was held at Compiègne, a forest in Northern France. This was the same location where the Germans signed the armistice that ended World War I. After the signing in World War I, Hitler had the railway carriage it occurred in taken to Germany and destroyed. He also had the site itself completely cleared. He wanted no further reminders that Germany had lost the First World War.

Q: What was Black Thursday?

A: On August 15, 1940, the Luftwaffe was conducting bombing raids over Britain. They expanded their reach past London to try to hit more targets. The Luftwaffe lost 69 planes and 190 crew members that day. The Germans called that day "Black Thursday." Partly based on that loss, the Luftwaffe narrowed its targeting to just seven sectors of London moving forward.

Q: How did the Germans use radio beams to target the British city of Coventry?

A: In late 1940, Germany started using a special system called *X-Verfahren*. This sent four radio beams over Britain that formed an X. Their aircraft had special equipment that allowed them to detect the beams. The X was targeted over Coventry. The planes followed the beams to the center of the X and dropped the bombs there.

A: On April 8, 1940, British Royal Navy Lieutenant Commander Gerard Roope was the commander of the *Glowworm*, a destroyer that was in the North Sea near Norway. The ship was acting as an escort for another ship that was placing mines. The *Glowworm* faced two German destroyers that were escorting a cruiser ship. The cruiser was the *Admiral von Hipper*, commanded by Captain Hellmuth Heye.

The *Glowworm* and the German destroyers fired at each other, and one of the German ships went down. The *Hipper* then began firing at the *Glowworm*. The *Glowworm* was hit and was on fire. Captain Roope knew that his ship was going down, but he decided to continue to fight the Germans to do as much damage as he could before he went down.

He fired torpedoes at the *Hipper*, but they all missed. He then drove the *Glowworm* directly into the *Hipper*. It made a hole in the *Hipper*. Captain Roope then ordered his men to abandon the sinking *Glowworm*. The Germans attempted to rescue the seamen from the water. Captain Roope grabbed hold of a rope, but let go out of exhaustion before he could be rescued. Captain Roope died along with 111 members of his crew that day. The *Hipper* rescued 31 men who survived. Captain Heye told the men they were very brave. He later sent a message through the Red Cross to the British War Office, recommending Captain Roope for the Victoria Cross, Britain's highest combat medal. For the medal to be awarded, a regimental-level office and three witnesses had to make the recommendation. Because there were no surviving British officers from the event, the War Office accepted Heye's recommendation since he was an officer. Roope was awarded the medal after his death. It is one of the few times a medal has been awarded based on the recommendation of the enemy.

Q: When did Italy enter the war?

A: Italy entered the war by declaring war on France on June 10, 1940. This wasn't a bold move since Germany was clearly going to be victorious over France. Mussolini, Italy's leader, was able to claim a 50-mile zone of France as Italy's.

Q: Why did Italy invade Greece?

A: Germany announced it was occupying Romania. Mussolini was upset that he hadn't been told in advance by his German allies. He then announced he was going to occupy Greece. Italy invaded Greece on October 28, 1940. Within two months the Greeks had pushed Italy out. The invasion was not successful.

Q: How did the Norwegian royal family escape the Nazis?

A: On April 9, 1940, Germany sent a ship into Oslofjord to capture the Norwegian royal family. A fort was able to sink the ship using torpedoes. The royal family escaped and fled the country.

Q: What tactic did German U-boats use to evade detection by the British in the Battle of the Atlantic?

A: U-boats sank many Allied ships in 1940. The British Royal Navy used sonar to detect the U-boats when they were underwater. However, when a U-boat was on the surface, it could not be located by sonar. The Royal Navy was beginning to use radar, but this early in the war, it was not fully in use. German U-boats would surface at night or in bad weather and get close to British ships without being seen. This allowed them to do surprise attacks.

Q: Which medical invention saved thousands of lives during the war?

A: In 1940 Edwin Cohn, a Harvard biochemist, figured out how to remove plasma from human blood and store it for long periods of time. This discovery allowed for the collection and storage of plasma, which could be shipped to the frontline troops and field hospitals. When a soldier was wounded, he would lose a lot of blood. Blood plasma could be given to the patient to replace the lost blood and save his life. Because there are no red blood cells in plasma, blood type does not matter, so any plasma could be used for any patient. Blood plasma was used at Pearl Harbor.

Q: How did a British agent steal diamonds from underneath the Nazis' noses?

A: Germany began invading the Netherlands in May 1940. Amsterdam was the center of the diamond business, and most of the world's diamonds were kept there. Industrial diamonds were important for manufacturing, and the Germans wanted them to help them build trucks, weapons, and radar machines. Lieutenant Colonel Montagu Chidson was sent by the British to get the diamonds before the Nazis could. Chidson got a key to a building with a safe full of diamonds. He still had to get the combination lock open. He tried and tried, and just as the Germans were entering the building, he cracked the code. Chidson got out of the country on his own and made his way back to Britain. He gave the diamonds to the Dutch queen.

Q: Why did the British sink some French navy ships in French Algeria?

A: On July 3, 1940, there were French ships at Mers El Kébir on the coast of French Algeria. France had surrendered to Germany a few days before this incident. The British determined that the Germans could gain an advantage if they could control these ships (five battleships and six destroyers, as well as some other ships). Under the armistice France signed with Germany, Germany was not allowed to use the French navy. The British did not trust the Germans to keep their word. The British gave the French admiral in control of the ships four choices. They could join the British navy, they could sail the ships to British ports, they could sail the ships to a nearby British base where they would be immobilized, or they could sink their own ships. The French did not respond, so the British attacked. Taking those ships out of commission prevented the Germans from using the ships in the war.

Q: What was the Battle of Switzerland?

A: This question might seem confusing since Switzerland was neutral in World War II. Despite this, Switzerland did actually engage with both the Axis and Allied forces. Hitler had a plan to invade Switzerland but never carried it out. Although Switzerland officially didn't take sides in the war, it was economically dependent on Germany. And it was eventually surrounded on all sides by Axis-controlled countries.

Once the Germans moved against the Allies, the Germans began to fly through Swiss airspace to get to France. Beginning in May of 1940, there were several air battles between the Germans and the Swiss. The Swiss shot down

11 German planes over their airspace. Three Swiss planes were shot down by the Germans.

The Germans said that their planes entered Swiss airspace by mistake. They wanted the Swiss to apologize for shooting them down. They threatened to retaliate if the Swiss refused. The Swiss apologized for possible border violations by their pilots and ordered their planes not to engage with foreign planes. Also in 1940 the British RAF mistakenly bombed the Swiss cities of Basel and Zurich, but the damage was not severe.

The Swiss remained out of the war until 1943. The Americans bombed Samedan, Switzerland, in October. Then in April 1944, the Americans bombed the city of Schaffhausen, which is near the German border. One hundred people died and there was significant damage to the city. The Swiss considered this a deliberate attack. The Americans apologized and blamed the weather for the mistake. The winds were extremely strong that day, so the pilots flew much farther than they anticipated, ending up over Switzerland when they thought they were over Germany.

However, the Americans continued to attack other parts of Switzerland. Throughout the war, the Swiss killed 20 British Royal Air Force members and 16 American airmen. They attacked 21 American bombers that landed in Switzerland. Americans captured in Switzerland were held in internment camps in terrible conditions, and the Swiss refused to allow the Red Cross to deliver packages to them. More than 1,000 Americans were held as POWs.

Q: Which children's author crashed his plane in the war and survived?

A: Roald Dahl, later known for books such as *Charlie and the Chocolate Factory*, *James and the Giant Peach*, and *Matilda*, joined the British RAF and became an aircraft man. He was assigned to fly a Gloster Gladiator without being trained for it. On September 19, 1940, he flew from Abu Seir to Mersa Matruh, Egypt. When he landed, he was running low on fuel and couldn't see the landing strip. He landed in the desert. His plane hit a boulder and crashed. He survived but later suffered from headaches and was taken out of combat.

Q: Did the Germans ever fight in the Pacific Ocean?

A: Although the Germans were mostly engaged in war in the Atlantic, they did venture into the Pacific. In 1940, German ships sunk Allied ships near New Zealand to prevent shipments of phosphate to Australia. Phosphate is an important ingredient in fertilizer.

Q: What do today's Purple Hearts have to do with World War II?

A: In 1945, the Allies were deciding to either invade Japan or drop the nuclear bomb. An invasion was predicted to lose 1 million Allied troops (and 10 million Japanese citizens). Because there was such a high potential for the loss of life, the American military began to produce hundreds of thousands of Purple Heart awards, so they would be ready if and when massive amounts of American troops were killed or injured. Ultimately, the Allies chose not to invade, and the nuclear bomb ended the war. The US did not need all the Purple Heart awards it produced. There is still a stockpile of these medals, and the ones that are given out today were produced during World War II.

1941

The year 1941 brought good news and bad news for the Allied forces. Hitler's bombing of Britain in the Battle of Britain was unsuccessful and Germany was not able to take Britain. However, three countries joined the Axis alliance (Bulgaria, Romania, and Hungary). Germany took Yugoslavia and Greece and then invaded the Soviet Union. The United States entered the war when Japan bombed Pearl Harbor. Germany declared war against the US. With the bombing of Pearl Harbor, the war in the Pacific began.

Q: Who was the most decorated female veteran of World War II?

A: Colonel Ruby Bradley was serving in the US Army Nurse Corps as head nurse at Camp John Hay in the Philippines in December 1944. Soon after the Japanese bombed Pearl Harbor, they bombed Camp John Hay. Bradley and other nurses escaped and walked 18 miles to a logging camp, where they were captured by the Japanese. Bradley was held as a prisoner of war in two different internment camps. She and other nurses created a hospital where they cared for the other prisoners. She helped deliver 13 babies and assisted in 230 surgeries. She also hid food in her pockets to feed the hungry children in the camp. When she was rescued in February 1945, she weighed 88 pounds and had nearly starved to death. She received many medals and honors for her service, including a Bronze Star and a Legion of Merit.

Q: How did one sailor change the navy's segregation policy?

A: In 1941, Black soldiers and naval officers were not allowed to train for combat. They were assigned to segregated units and required to do work behind the scenes. When Pearl Harbor was attacked on December 7, 1941, Mess Attendant Second Class Doris (Dorie) Miller was below deck doing laundry on the American battleship *West Virginia*. When the ship was hit, he first carried his wounded

Dorie Miller being awarded the Navy Cross.

captain to safety. Then he reported to the ship's guns where he was supposed to feed ammunition into the machine guns.

One of the guns did not have anyone firing it, so Miller stepped in. Without any training he began firing it. He continued firing until the order was given to abandon ship. Then he rescued several sailors who had fallen into the burning water. He swam to the shore, dodging bullets. History is unclear about how many planes he shot down, but it is believed his bravery took down two or more Japanese planes.

His role is important not just because he saved lives and was brave enough to fire a gun he had not been trained to use. Several of his crewmates were awarded Medals of Honor for their bravery that day but he was not. He was later awarded the Navy Cross, which is not as high of an honor. This sparked an important conversation about race and what role Black men should be allowed to perform in the armed services. By April of 1942, the navy allowed Black men who enlisted to be trained to use guns, radar, and other special items previously reserved only for white sailors.

Sadly, Miller was killed on the USS *Liscome Bay* by a torpedo attack by the Japanese in 1943. In 1944, the navy finally began to allow Black men to train as officers. In 1973, a destroyer (*Miller*) was named in his honor. Currently there are eight Black admirals in the US Navy. His heroism was directly responsible for the end of segregation in the navy.

Q: What was the last radio message from the *Bismarck*?

A: The 42,000-ton battleship *Bismarck* was launched by the German navy on May 18, 1941, in the North Sea. The British sent the battleship *Prince of Wales* and the HMS *Hood* battle cruiser after it. The *Hood* was attacked by the *Bismarck* and sunk. The *Prince of Wales* fired at the *Bismarck* and hit her fuel tanks. The

Bismarck decided to head back for repairs. Torpedo planes were sent after her and broke her rudder. Because of this, she could only go in circles! The British battleships *King George V* and *Rodney* came in for the kill and sank her, but not until the ship sent a final message. "We shall fight to the last shell. Long live the Führer," was the last radio message sent by the German battleship *Bismarck*.

Q: What were "wolf packs" during the Battle of the Atlantic?

A: Before 1941, German U-boats operated individually, mostly attacking merchant ships on the Atlantic Ocean. After 1941, Allied merchant ships began sailing in groups, called convoys, with escorts and air support. In response, the Germans started to use a strategy the British called "wolf packs." One U-boat would follow a ship and then call others in by radio. The U-boats would form a group and attack the ships at night by surfacing and firing at them.

Q: How did a lack of fuel almost ruin a winning British strategy?

A: In July 1941, the British were trying to capture Syria in order to control the bridges over the Euphrates River. British Major General William Slim came up with a plan to control the enemy, the Vichy French forces (these were the French who were controlled by the Germans). He planned to send one brigade to the enemy on the south and then send another to circle around them and take the position to their north. This plan would give the British control over one of the bridges. The night before, an aide woke him up to tell him that they were almost out of fuel. Slim almost cancelled the dual plan in favor of a singular attack. However, he decided to try the double-prong approach. He ordered the officers to drain the gasoline out of every vehicle and use it for the vehicles they needed for the plan. There was just enough fuel to do it once, and if they ran out, they would lose. On July 3, the British carried out the plan and the Vichy French fled, leaving behind all their fuel. The British took the bridge and the Vichy French surrendered eight days later.

Q: What were the Doolittle Raids?

A: After the bombing of Pearl Harbor, Jimmy Doolittle (who later became a general) came up with an idea for an air raid over Tokyo. The secret plan involved moving 16 B-25 Mitchell bombers near Japan aboard the USS *Hornet*.

B-25 Mitchell

The planes then took off on a short runway—the first time that had ever been attempted. They flew over Japan, dropping bombs, and crash-landed in China. Three of the pilots died and eight were captured. All the planes were lost, but the Doolittle Raids were viewed as act of bravery, ingenuity, and courage.

Q: How did radar almost prevent the bombing of Pearl Harbor?

A: An hour before the attack at Pearl Harbor, a mobile radar station on Oahu reported approaching aircraft. The radar operators' commanders dismissed their report and believed that they were inexperienced and mistaken. If the report had been taken seriously, the entire course of the war in the Pacific could have been completely different.

Q: What was the first military engagement between the US and Germany?

A: On September 4, 1941, before the US had entered the war, the USS *Greer* was transporting passengers and mail to Iceland. A British plane alerted *Greer* that there was a U-boat nearby. *Greer* followed the U-boat. The British plane dropped bombs and then left. Then the U-boat shot a torpedo at *Greer*. *Greer* responded with depth charges. The U-boat fired another torpedo. *Greer* released more depth charges. The ships parted ways. *Greer* was the first US ship to engage with a U-boat.

Q: How did artificial legs save a pilot's life?

A: British RAF pilot Douglas Bader lost his legs when his plane crashed in an accident in 1931. He was fitted with two metal prosthetic legs. This didn't stop him from signing up to fight in World War II. He was allowed to enlist and flew a Supermarine Spitfire fighter plane. He shot down a German plane in 1939 and was promoted to commander of his squadron. In August of 1939, the squadron took down twelve Axis aircraft. Bader shot down two of those himself. He's credited with coming up with a strategy called "the Big Wing formation." Multiple squadrons would all take off at the same time, then meet up in the sky and attack the Germans together like one unit. By the end of the war, he was the RAF pilot who had shot down the fifth most enemy planes.

In 1941, Bader was flying over France on a daylight mission. In August, his plane either collided with a German plane or was shot down by friendly fire (when a soldier's own countrymen mistakenly fire at them in the confusion of war). Bader tried to bail out of the plane, but his right prosthetic leg was stuck. The strap holding it onto his body broke and he was able to parachute out of the plane, saving his life. If he'd had two real legs, he would have been trapped and crashed with his plane, almost certainly dying. But because his prosthetic leg came off, he was able to parachute out of the plane.

He was captured by the Germans and held as a POW. His prosthetic leg was found in the wreckage and returned to him while he was in a POW hospital in occupied France. After he recovered, he was held in captivity. He filled his hollow legs with dirt and sand when he and his fellow captives dug to create escape tunnels. He also filled the legs with food he would smuggle in. At one point, he needed a replacement leg, and the Germans offered safe passage to any plane flying one in for him. The Allied forces used that opportunity to fly in a bomber to drop the leg and some bombs as well. He was rescued in 1945 and was knighted in 1976. He went on to fly commercial planes and passed away in 1982.

Q: Which Atlantic island nation did the United States occupy during the war?

A: Iceland was part of Denmark at the start of the war. Once the Germans took over Denmark in 1940, Iceland formed its own government. But it had no navy and no army. Churchill said, "Whoever possesses Iceland holds a pistol firmly pointed at England, America, and Canada." Britain was very concerned that Germany could take control of Iceland and then the Atlantic. Because of this, Britain took control of Iceland in 1940. By spring of 1941, Britain needed all her troops to defend her own country. Britain asked the United States to take over protecting Iceland. The US Marines were sent to occupy Iceland.

Q: What was the Continuation War?

A: The Soviet Union invaded Finland in 1939 and took territory (see page 32). In 1941, Germany invaded the Soviet Union, and Finland joined forces with the Germans to try to get back the territory taken by the Soviets. This was called "the Continuation War."

Q: Why did Rommel wear goggles on his hat?

A: German field marshal Erwin Rommel commanded German troops in the war in Africa. Because of his winning streak and his technique of leading his troops from the front instead of behind, he was called "the Desert Fox." Rommel was often seen with a pair of goggles on his hat. In 1941 in Libya, Rommel had dinner with one of the British prisoners of war, Major General Michael Gambier-Parry. It was not unusual for military leaders

Rommel and his well-known goggles

to be friendly with opposing leaders they had captured. Gambier-Parry complained to Rommel that one of the Germans had taken his hat. Rommel issued orders for the hat to be returned. He then found Gambier-Parry's goggles being used by the Germans and asked him if he could keep them. He wore them on his hat frequently. Rommel committed suicide in 1944 after helping with a plot to that attempted to assassinate Hitler.

Q: Why did the Blitz end?

A: Germany's nighttime bombing raids on London reached a high point on May 10, 1941. On that night, the raids destroyed one-third of London's streets and killed 1,400 civilians. Britain wasn't about to surrender though. Hitler had to send two-thirds of his Luftwaffe to fight against the Soviet Union and could not keep up the pressure on Britain. The Blitz had ended, but occasional bombing raids continued throughout the war.

Q: What was the Afrika Korps?

A: Italy had territories in Africa before the war began. Once Italy was involved in the war, it wanted to gain more territory in Africa to help it control the Mediterranean. In 1940, Italy invaded Egypt and was stopped by Allied forces. Italy had to retreat. Germany was allied with Italy and needed to support it. In early 1941 Hitler created the Afrika Korps, a group of forces sent to Africa to fight with Italy against Allied forces. General Rommel was put in charge of these forces.

Q: Which sports fields did Iraqis use to fight the British in the war?

A: In 1941, Iraq had a monarchy that was backed by the British. However, it was overthrown by pro-Germans. This meant that Britain wouldn't have access to Iraq's oil, which it needed for fuel during the war. British forces landed at Basra and tried to take the base there. The Iraqis converted the base's polo field and golf course into extra airfields so they could fly more planes. The Iraqis were not prepared to battle the British and soon gave up the base.

Q: Which German victory convinced Hitler to stop using paratroopers for sneak attacks?

A: In May 1941, Germany was battling for control of the island of Crete. Germany sent paratroopers in to take the island. The paratroopers had few supplies and only the weapons they could carry. They fought against New Zealand, part of the Allied Forces, which was trying to hold the island. A communication mistake led New Zealand to withdraw from part of the island. The Germans captured the city of Maleme because of this. However, 400 out of 600 German troops were killed. This massacre led Hitler to decide never to send paratroopers in alone again. After this, he only used them as support for ground troops.

Q: How many horses did the Germans use when invading the Soviet Union?

A: Germany invaded the Soviet Union in Operation Barbarossa on June 22, 1941. Germany had assembled the largest military force ever used. Three million soldiers invaded. Among the millions of soldiers, Germany also used horses. They brought 625,000 horses as part of the invasion.

Q: How did weather protect Moscow from invasion?

A: Hitler ordered his troops to march on Moscow in what was called "Operation Typhoon" in the fall of 1941. They got within 90 miles of Moscow when the autumn rains started, turning the roads to mud. By November, winter had come and the ground was frozen. Many troops suffered from frostbite. Some tanks would not run in the cold weather. Germany was forced to retreat and did not capture Moscow.

Q: When did Hitler first order mass killings?

A: Although the Germans killed thousands of Jewish people in Poland and put many others into work camps, Hitler had not yet issued orders for mass murder. That changed in March 1941. Hitler issued a Commissar Order that directed mass murders of Jewish people and communists as Germany invaded the Soviet Union. German records show 600,000 Jewish people were murdered in 1941 by Germans in the Soviet Union. Soviet troops were also killed. Nearly 3 million Soviet troops died at the hands of the Germans in the war.

Q: What was the first American ship sunk in the war?

A: Although the United States had not officially entered the war, it was using ships to accompany supply ships to Britain. On October 31, 1941, The USS *Reuben James* was hit by a U-boat and sunk. Ninety-three men on board the ship were killed.

Q: What method of transportation helped the Japanese take Malaya?

A: Hours before the attack on Pearl Harbor, the Japanese actually began the war in the Pacific by invading Malaya, a peninsula in southeast Asia. The Japanese had the element of surprise. They also used an unusual type of transportation. They chose to use bicycles. This let their soldiers move quickly and quietly. They could go down narrow roads and even carry the bikes over rivers. They could carry twice as much weight as a soldier on foot was able to. They didn't bring the bicycles with them though. In the years before the war, Japan had exported and sold bicycles to Malaya. They confiscated those bikes after they landed. The Allies tried to stop the Japanese by putting holes in their tires. The Japanese just took the tires off and rode on the bare rims. The noise this made on the road sounded like tanks were approaching and scared the Allied troops.

Q: When did Britain declare war on Japan?

A: Britain entered the war in 1939 against Germany. However, Britain did not declare war on Japan until December 8, 1941.

Q: How many Americans died in the attack on Pearl Harbor?

A: The Japanese attack was planned for a Sunday when many soldiers were on leave. The Americans were not expecting an attack at Pearl Harbor and had many aircraft out in the open, unprotected. The anti-aircraft guns were not manned. The Japanese flew in with 366 bombers and sunk the USS *Arizona* and damaged seven other battleships. More than 300 planes were destroyed or damaged. The Americans lost 2,403 people. The Japanese lost only 55 men and 29 planes in the attack.

Rescuing survivors from the attack on Pearl Harbor, December 7, 1941

Q: What was the first Japanese vessel sunk by the Americans in the war?

A: Although it has generally been believed that the Americans did not attack the Japanese until after the attack on Pearl Harbor, in fact an American ship did sink a Japanese sub before the attack. At 6:30 a.m. on December 7, 1941 (the Pearl Harbor attack began at 7:55 a.m. that day), the USS *Ward* was notified that there was a suspicious vessel near Pearl Harbor. It was a Japanese midget submarine. The *Ward* fired on the sub and sunk it. This was the first shot fired against the Japanese. The pilot was the first Japanese casualty of the war. This fact was unknown for many years until the submarine was recovered in 2002 by a Hawaiian research lab diving in the area.

Q: When did the draft begin in the United States for World War II?

A: When the war began, the United States Army was smaller than Portugal's army. On September 16, 1941, before the United States entered the war, President Roosevelt signed the Selective Training and Service Act. It was the first peacetime draft in the US and required all men aged 21 to 45 to register. After Pearl Harbor was bombed, the law was changed to require men ages 18 to 64 to register. Ten million men were drafted during the war. The draft remained in place until 1973.

Q: Who was the only German POW to escape from Canada and rejoin the war?

A: Franz von Werra served in the German Luftwaffe and was shot down over Britain and captured. He attempted to escape several times. Once he used a pickaxe to attack a guard. Another time he snuck away while outside. A more successful attempt involved digging a tunnel and putting on the uniform of a Dutch pilot, convincing a train conductor to give him a ride, and being questioned by police but fooling them. He was eventually caught and sent to Canada to be held in a POW camp there. On a train on the way to the camp, he jumped out a window. He was not captured this time. He walked across a frozen river into the United States where the German consulate helped him cross the border to Mexico. He went to Brazil, Spain, and Italy and made it back to Germany in 1941. He was awarded the Knight's Cross and went back into active service. His plane crashed and he was never found.

Q: How did Stalin's son end up in the hands of the Germans?

A: Yakov Dzhugashvili was the son of Joseph Stalin, the leader of the Soviet Union. Yakov and his father did not get along. The son married a Jewish woman. He was a commander in the Red Army at the Battle of Smolensk in 1941. For years it was believed he was captured by the Germans, but recent evidence has shown it was likely he surrendered to them. Once he was in German hands, he was very critical of the Soviet Union. Stalin put his son's wife in prison and tortured

Yakov Dzhugashvili

her. In 1943 at the Battle of Stalingrad, the Germans offered to trade Yakov for Germans held by the Soviets. Stalin refused. Yakov died in 1943 in a German concentration camp when he electrocuted himself on a fence.

Q: Who was Lady Death?

A: Women were not allowed to fight on the front lines for the United States, but the Soviet Union trained women to be snipers (soldiers who shoot from long distances using rifles). Lyudmila Pavlichenko, called "Lady Death," fought in the Siege of Odessa and the Siege of Sevastopol in 1941. She is the most successful female sniper in history. She had 309 confirmed kills. She went on to train other Soviet snipers.

Q: Which airman climbed out onto the wing of a plane during flight to save it?

A: New Zealander Sergeant James Ward was second pilot of a Wellington bomber on a flight from Germany back to Britain. It was attacked by a German Messerschmitt Bf 110. His plane was hit and a fire started on a wing. The crew tried to put it out, even throwing their coffee at it. They couldn't put out the fire. Ward had his crew tie him to the plane. Then, as the plane was flying, he crawled out onto the wing. He used his hands to make holes in the wing as he crawled so he had handholds. He used a piece of canvas to put out the fire. He pulled on the rope to pull himself back into the plane. He was awarded the Victoria Cross for his bravery.

1942

The war in the Pacific was difficult and challenging for the Allied forces. In 1942 the Japanese had victories in Guam and the Philippines. However, the Battle of Midway was a turning point, with Allied forces claiming a victory over Japan. There was also good news in Europe. Germany was prevented from taking the Soviet Union and began to retreat. The Allied forces invaded Northern Africa and fought the Germans there.

Q: Was United States land ever occupied by another country during World War II?

A: Yes. While the Japanese bombed Pearl Harbor but never actually occupied it, most people don't know that Japanese troops did take control of two islands off the coast of Alaska. The islands are called Attu and Kiska. The Japanese landed on the islands in June of 1942, six months after Pearl Harbor, and occupied them. In 1943, in the Battle of the Aleutian Islands, the Americans set up a blockade so the Japanese soldiers couldn't get supplies. American and Japanese ships fought on the sea, and then Americans took back Attu Island on foot. This was the only World War II land battle that ever happened on American soil. Americans then took over Kiska, only to find the Japanese had already left.

Aerial photo of a US Army Air Forces attack on Kiska island.

Q: What was the bloodiest battle in the entire history of the world?

A: The Battle of Stalingrad, which lasted from 1942 to 1943, was the battle with the most deaths and injuries. Two million people died or were injured. During this battle, the Germans attempted to capture the Russian city of Stalingrad. The Russians won that battle and the Germans were forced to withdraw from Stalingrad. This was a turning point in the war, and an important loss for the Germans.

Q: Who were the *Malgré-nous*?

A: After Germany invaded France, it essentially controlled France and everyone in the country. When the Germans needed more soldiers to fight in the war, they forced Frenchmen to join their army in 1942. If a man refused to join, his family was deported (removed from the country). These forced French soldiers called themselves *Malgré-nous*, which means "against our will" in French. After the war, some of these men were tried by France and convicted for assisting the Germans. The French government eventually gave them amnesty (an official pardon).

Q: Which battle was fought against no one?

A: On February 23, 1942, a Japanese submarine surfaced near Santa Barbara, California, and fired at an oil refinery. Because of this, California was on high alert. Two days later, radar picked up something in the skies near Los Angeles and alarms went off. Troops began shooting anti-aircraft guns into the sky. They fought for an hour and used 1,400 rounds of ammunition. Everyone thought LA was under attack. It turned out there was nothing there and the Americans were shooting for no reason. However, the shooting damaged buildings and homes, and five people died from heart attacks and car accidents caused by the scare. This was called "the Battle of Los Angeles" even though there was no actual enemy.

Q: **What was the secret to the Americans defeating Japan in the Battle of Midway?**

A: The Japanese defeated the Americans at Pearl Harbor because they had the element of surprise. No one knew Japan was going to attack the United States. By the Battle of Midway in 1942, the Americans had developed a team of code breakers (called "Station Hypo") who were so fast they could intercept and decode a Japanese message within hours. The code breakers believed that the Japanese used AF to mean Midway Atoll (a group of islands in the south Pacific with an American base) in their messages, but they weren't positive.

The code breakers got a message that Japan planned to attack AF. The leaders in Washington wanted to be sure that the code breakers were right and that "AF" meant Midway. They set a trap. They had the base on Midway send a radio message to Pearl Harbor that the machines on the base that created fresh water had broken. They then intercepted a Japanese message that the fresh water machine on AF was broken. They were then sure that AF meant Midway, and that the Japanese were planning to attack it.

The US sent three aircraft carriers to the area and were able to surprise the Japanese when they attacked. The Japanese were defeated. This battle was an important turning point for the Allied forces in the south Pacific.

Q: What did the saying "a man a mile" mean?

A: Because China was an ally against Japan, the United States worked hard to support China in the Pacific theater. This meant making sure China could get supplies. The Japanese occupied Burma in 1942, making it hard to get supplies through to China. To get supplies through, the US started building a road from India to China. The road was 1,079 miles long. It was built in the mountains. Fifteen thousand soldiers were assigned to work building the road. They often worked under enemy fire, and 1,133 men died. Because of this they said the road cost them "a man a mile." For each mile of road that was built, at least one soldier died.

Q: How difficult was it for reporters to take photos at the front lines?

A: In 1942 the US established the Army Pictorial Service (APS). This was set up so that the army could get photos and videos of what was happening during the war. Each member was given a camera, called a "Speed Graphic." There were many pieces to each camera including lenses, film, flashbulbs, and tripods. There were 11 steps the photographer had to go through, from opening the camera to taking the photo, which made it very challenging to capture action on the battlefield.

Q: What was V-mail?

A: There was a huge amount of mail sent to and from servicemen in the war. In 1945, 2.5 billion pieces of mail went through the Army Postal Service and 8 million through the navy. Because there was so much mail, in 1942, the military created the V-mail or Victory Mail system. Forms were filled out instead of letters. Each person could get two forms per day from the post office. They were then photographed on microfilm and sent overseas. Thirty-seven bags of regular mail could be condensed into one bag of V-mail. The mail was then printed once it arrived overseas and given to the soldiers. This allowed more mail to get to the troops much faster. Senders couldn't include anything with the letter (like photographs). Women sometimes would leave lipstick kisses on mail to men they loved, but doing this would get the lipstick on the scanning machines and cause paper jams.

Q: **Which submarine was always greeted with stacks of toilet paper, toilet paper streamers, and toilet paper necklaces?**

A: The USS *Skipjack*, a salmon-class submarine, patrolled the Pacific and was the first US submarine to attack an enemy aircraft carrier and destroyer with torpedoes. However, the crew was suffering from a very important shortage. In 1941 the ship requested 150 rolls of toilet paper. A letter was received in return that said "cancelled—cannot identify." Lieutenant Commander James Coe wrote a famous reply explaining what they needed and included a sample. He said that the crew was using excess Navy paperwork as toilet paper in the meantime, joking that they were doing their part to reduce excess paperwork. He explained that the situation was now dire and said, "In order to cooperate in our war effort at a small local sacrifice, the *Skipjack* desires no further action be taken until the end of the current war, which has created a situation aptly described as 'war is hell.'" When the sub returned to base in Australia, she was greeted with huge stacks of toilet paper, the docks were decorated with toilet paper streamers, and the dock crew wore toilet paper necklaces. Every time she returned to port during the war, she was greeted in this same way. This story was later told in the movie *Operation Petticoat,* starring Cary Grant.

A: In 1942, the US military established Dogs for Defense, a new program to train dogs to help in battle. Of the 18,000 dogs in the unit, many were volunteered by their owners. The program promised to return the dogs to their owners

Two sentry dogs being trained for guard duty

after the war. Dogs had to be between 14 months and three and a half years old to qualify. At first only purebred dogs were allowed, but soon mixed breeds were accepted. The German shepherd was named by the War Department as the official US Army dog.

War dog training

Dogs first underwent medical testing. Then they were tested for intelligence. Once they passed that, they were sent for military training with the army or marines. The dogs were initially taught basic obedience and hand signals. It was important that a dog learned to obey commands like stay so they could be trusted to hold still when near the enemy. They had to learn not to bark or make noises. They ran obstacle courses and learned to swim. They were taught to wear gas masks and to ride in Jeeps. They also had to learn not to be afraid of gunfire.

Dogs were trained to do specific jobs, and the jobs were breed specific. Breeds like Dobermans, German shepherds, and collies were used as scouts. Huskies and malamutes were used as sled dogs. Newfoundlands and Saint Bernards were used as pack dogs. The dogs were very important in combat.

Chips, a German shepherd and Siberian husky mix, charged a hut with Italian soldiers, dragged one out by the neck, and forced three others to surrender to the American troops. He received a Purple Heart and Silver Star for his bravery, but then those awards were taken away when the military decided those awards could only be given to humans. He famously bit the hand of General Eisenhower (who later became president) when he petted him. A comic and books were written about him.

At the end of the war, there were 559 US Marine dogs alive, and 540 were returned to their owners after being trained to return to civilian life.

Q: The crew of which ship survived in lifeboats for 20 days after their ship was sunk?

A: The US merchant ship *Paul Luckenbach* set sail from South Africa on September 7, 1942. The ship was in the Indian Ocean when a Japanese submarine hit it with torpedoes. The surviving crew got into four lifeboats. They rowed across the Indian Ocean for 20 days before they got to India. They traveled over 800 miles to make it to safety.

Q: How was a sailor saved by his mother during the Battle of Guadalcanal?

A: Navy Signalman Elgin Staples was serving on the USS *Astoria* during the Battle of Guadalcanal on August 8, 1942. The *Astoria* was hit by Japanese cruisers. Staples was hit in the legs with shrapnel, thrown into the air, and landed in the water. A rubber life belt he was wearing kept him afloat until he was rescued. Staples went back to the *Astoria* to try to help the crew. *Astoria* sank and Staples ended up back in the water. He still had his life belt on and was rescued again. Two hundred men aboard the Astoria died in the attack.

Staples was from Akron, Ohio, and his life belt was made by the Firestone company in Akron, Ohio. When he returned home, he told his mother that he was saved by a life belt made by that company, which she happened to work for. He still had the life belt and showed it to her. The numbers stamped inside showed it was a life belt she had personally inspected as part of her job. Her work had saved her own son.

Q: When did the first Code Talkers begin their work in the war?

A: Code Talkers were Native Americans who used the Navajo language (an unwritten language) as a code. This code was unbreakable since no other country knew the Navajo language. Native Americans were recruited for the program beginning in 1940. By 1942 the first Code Talkers completed their training. More than 400 Native American men from 16 different tribes participated in the program. The Marine Corps created a special code-talking school to train them. The Code Talkers were present at many important battles including Utah Beach and Iwo Jima. Six Code Talkers worked at Iwo Jima, transmitting over 800 messages. None of their messages contained any errors.

The code they used included existing words in the Navajo language as well as words they made up. There is no word for "submarine" in Navajo, so they used the words for "iron" and "fish" together as code. For "ship" they used the words for "houses on the water." The word for "tank" was the word for "turtle." They also agreed on one Navajo animal that would represent each letter of the English alphabet, such as the Navajo word for "ant," which was used to represent the letter *A*. The code eventually included 411 terms.

The Code Talkers worked in teams during battles. They were responsible for carrying and setting up radio communication equipment on the battlefield. At one location, one Code Talker would be given a message to transmit. He would translate it into Navajo without writing anything down. His partner would send the radio message. On the other end, one man would receive the radio message. The other would translate it from Navajo into English. They could transmit a message in two and a half minutes.

The work the Code Talkers did remained secret until 1968 when the program was declassified. Since then, all the Code Talkers have been awarded the Congressional Medal of Honor.

Code Talkers being sworn into service

Q: How many Japanese aircraft carriers were taken out during the Battle of Midway?

A: Four. The Japanese had six aircraft carriers. When the Allies took out four of them, this left them with only two. This eventually contributed to their loss in the war.

Q: What was Hitler's plan for the citizens of Stalingrad?

A: Hitler planned to win the Battle of Stalingrad. If the battle was won, he had orders in place for every single man in the city to be executed. All women and children were to be deported. Fortunately, the Soviet Union won this important battle and Hitler's plans were never carried out.

Q: What was the strategy of island-hopping?

A: Once Japan attacked Pearl Harbor, the American forces fought hard to gain control of the Pacific. This was difficult, though, since much of the fleet had been destroyed at Pearl Harbor. Once the Allies took Guadalcanal, they needed a strategy to take the rest of the Pacific. Fighting the Japanese on heavily fortified islands was too risky. Instead, the Americans developed a strategy called "island-hopping." They would take weakly defended islands and leave the Japanese alone on their fortified islands. This way they could begin to take control of the water and limit the supplies the Japanese could get. The Japanese were left alone on the fortified islands to die of starvation and illness.

Q: What was the Tokyo Express?

A: The Japanese navy brought in soldiers on ships each night to Guadalcanal. The Americans called these runs "the Tokyo

Express." Once the Allies gained ground in Guadalcanal, the Tokyo Express operated in reverse, taking 12,000 troops out of the area.

Q: **Why were marines based in Guadalcanal given machetes?**

A: Guadalcanal was a dense jungle. Marines needed machetes to cut through the vegetation to be able to advance. Sometimes it took troops two to three hours to cut through enough jungle to be able to move forward just a few yards.

Guadalcanal, August 1942

Q: **Which Japanese general drowned retreating from Port Moresby, New Guinea?**

A: The Japanese and Americans both recognized that New Guinea was an important area to take. Fighting began on June 22, 1942. Major General Tomitarō Horii commanded the Japanese troops as they fought against the Americans and Australians. The fighting was fierce and even though the Japanese outnumbered the Allies, Horii retreated. His superiors ordered him to move to another area and create a fortress. He drowned while trying to cross the Kumusi River.

Q: Why did Britain award the George Cross to the Island of Malta?

A: Malta, a British holding in the Mediterranean, was held under siege for two years, beginning in 1941. The British kept sending convoys to supply the troops and the people on the island, but Axis forces attacked them. Germany put mines in the water around Malta, making it nearly impossible for supplies to get through. In August 1942, the people were in danger of starving. Britain sent another convoy. Three of the ships finally made it to the island, including the tanker *Ohio*, which was carrying oil. The captain of the *Ohio* was given the George Cross for getting the ship through. Later that year King George IV gave another George Cross to the entire island for holding out and not giving up. It was the only time this medal was awarded to a group of people.

Q: What was the Leigh Light?

A: British forces were having trouble tracking German U-boats in the Battle of the Atlantic. The U-boats would surface at night when the British couldn't see them. They would appear on radar, but only within a certain range. Once they got out of range, the British had no idea where they went. In 1942, the British developed the Leigh Light to solve this problem. Once a U-boat was about to disappear on radar, the British ships would turn on a searchlight and keep it on the U-boat. Before the U-boat could go back underwater, bomber planes could attack it.

Q: How did Airey Neave manage to escape from a prisoner of war camp?

A: Neave was a British soldier serving in the Royal Artillery. He was wounded and tried to escape when he was captured in 1940 at Calais by the Germans. He made several attempts to escape but was always captured. He was finally sent to Colditz Castle, which had the highest level of security. In 1942 he made a German officer's uniform and wore it to walk right out of the camp. He first escaped through a trapdoor in the bottom of a stage during a play the prisoners were putting on. He took a train to Switzerland and made it home.

Q: Which general turned the US II Corps into a tough fighting force?

A: General George Patton assumed command of the US II Corps in March 1942 in Morocco. When he took over, he wrote in his diary that the corps was "a mess." He instituted tough new rules and training. He made the men stick to a strict code for their uniforms. He required them to shave every day. They had to leave their helmets on even while in the latrine (bathroom). They had to wear a tie—even in battle. Anyone who broke the rules was fined half a day's pay. Quickly, Patton turned the corps around, and by mid-1943 the corps pushed the Germans and Italians to surrender in Tunisia.

Q: What were the Baedeker Raids?

A: In 1942 Britain bombed the German cities of Lubeck and Rostock. These cities were primarily civilian targets. The wooden buildings burned quickly and 1,000 people died. In retaliation, Hitler began bombing tourist cities in England. He quickly bombed

Exeter, Bath, Norwich, Canterbury, and York. These cities were poorly defended. These were called the Baedeker Raids, named after a German tourism guide series that featured the cities.

Q: Which ship surprised the Japanese at the Battle of Midway?

A: The US aircraft carrier *Yorktown* was damaged during the Battle of the Coral Sea. The Japanese assumed it was out of commission. They were wrong. The *Yorktown* was taken to Pearl Harbor where it was repaired in only two days. *Yorktown* headed into the Battle of Midway, surprising the Japanese who didn't think the ship could fight.

The USS *Yorktown* is hit by a Japanese bomber in the Battle of Midway.

Q: When did the Americans fight against the French in the war?

A: Both the United States and France were part of the Allied forces in the war. However, Germany had set up a puppet government for the part of France they controlled. This was called the Vichy

French government (see page 58) and was part of the Axis forces. When the American forces joined the Allies in invading North Africa, Vichy French forces were some of the troops they faced.

Q: How did a man survive for 133 days on a raft after his ship was sunk by the Germans?

A: Poon Lim was a Chinese man who was working on the British merchant ship *Ben Lomond*. On November 23, 1942, the ship was sunk by a German U-boat. He was able to climb onto a raft and survive. He made a fishhook out of a piece of steel and made fishing line from a sack. He caught fish to eat. He also grabbed birds that landed on his raft. He gathered rainwater in a tarp and drank his own urine. He was able to survive for 133 days. He was rescued when the raft was found off the coast of Brazil.

Q: Which movie star did Hitler offer a reward for if captured?

A: American movie star Clark Gable (known for playing Rhett Butler in *Gone with the Wind*) enlisted in the military after his wife Carole Lombard was killed in a plane crash. He served as a second lieutenant in the Air Force. When Hitler found out Gable was serving, he offered a reward for anyone who captured Gable and brought the actor to him. Gable was never captured.

Q: Which soldier subdued three tanks with only a pistol?

A: Canadian Airborne Forces brigadier general James Hill was serving in Tunisia in 1942 when his group faced enemy tanks near the city of Beja. Three tanks had been dug into the side of a slope and were firing at his troops. Hill ran up to the first tank and stuck his pistol in the peephole and shot inside it. Italian soldiers came out and ran. He ran up to another tank and did the same thing. More Italian soldiers got out and fled. He went up to the third tank but its peephole was shut. So he banged on the turret with a stick. A German soldier leapt out and shot him in the chest, shoulder, and neck. Hill managed to kill the German. Hill was taken to a hospital and survived.

Q: How did a ship survive war with the Japanese by being disguised as a tropical island?

A: In 1942, the Dutch minesweeper ship *Abraham Crijnssen* was operating in the Java Sea and the Japanese were dominating the war. This ship was the last remaining Dutch ship that had not been sunk by the Japanese. The ship needed to get out of the area to safety in Australia but had to make it past the Japanese to do so. The crew stopped at one of the many islands in the area and began cutting down trees and vegetation. They covered the ship with them. During the day, the ship would stay anchored in one place and the Japanese would assume it was an island. At night it would sail closer to Australia. It arrived after eight days and safely escaped the Japanese.

Q: Where were the first German POWs captured by Americans?

A: The US Coast Guard boat *Icarus* was sailing from New York to Florida on May 8, 1942. They encountered U-boat *U-352* and sank it. They rescued 32 Germans from the water. These were the first German POWs held by the Americans in the war.

Q: How many German POWs were held in the US?

A: Between 1942 and 1945, 400,000 Germans were brought to the US to be held as prisoners of war. Five hundred POW camps were built to hold them. Many of these prisoners were put to work in factories and on farms and were paid for their work. Less than one percent attempted to escape, and of those who did, all were found. By 1946, all of them were returned to their home country.

Q: How did five brothers change military policy about siblings serving together?

A: Five brothers—George, Francis, Joseph, Madison, and Albert Sullivan—all enlisted together on the condition that they would be able to serve together. The US Navy assigned them to the USS *Juneau*. On November 14, 1942, the USS *Juneau* was sunk by the Japanese. All five of the Sullivan brothers died. Because of this, the military changed its rules about allowing members of the same family to serve together. The War Department also created the Sole Survivor Policy because of the Sullivan brothers. The law says that when there is one remaining child of a family, that child can request to be sent home. This prevents a family from losing all of its children in a war.

The five Sullivan Brothers

WWII BATTLE TRIVIA FOR KIDS

1943

In 1943, the Allied forces defeated Axis forces in Africa. The Allies then invaded Italy. Mussolini, Italy's dictator, was unseated. Italy joined the Allies to fight against Germany. The Allied forces continued to fight hard against Germany in Europe. The Battle of Berlin was begun. General Dwight D. Eisenhower was named Supreme Allied Commander. In the Pacific, the Americans gained control of Guadalcanal.

Q: What was the smelliest escape ever attempted during World War II?

A: Canadian Spitfire pilot Bill Ash was captured when his plane was shot down by the Germans over France in an air fight. His plane crashed and he survived. He was then held as a prisoner of war. In 1943, he and other servicemen dug an escape route down through the toilet and through a sewage tank and made it out. They were recaptured a few days later. Even though that stinky escape didn't work, Ash kept trying other escapes but was always captured. A movie was made about him, called *The Great Escape*, starring actor Steve McQueen.

Q: How was President Roosevelt almost killed by a torpedo?

A: On November 14, 1943, Roosevelt was on board the USS *Iowa*, going to an Allied military meeting in Tehran. The USS *William D. Porter* was escorting the ship. The crew was doing some training when they mistakenly fired a torpedo at the *Iowa*. The *Iowa* was able to steer away from it and the president was unharmed. The entire crew was ordered to Bermuda and arrested. Roosevelt commuted (reduced) the 14-year sentence its skipper received.

Q: Which army private had a song named after him for his bravery in the South Pacific?

A: The song "The Ballad of Rodger Young" was written by Frank Loesser about the heroics of American private Rodger Young who was serving on New Georgia Island in the South Pacific in July 1943. Young was sight- and hearing-impaired from an injury in high school. His platoon was attacking a hill held by the Japanese. Young was injured by Japanese machine-gun fire, but he refused to give up. His platoon started to back up, but Young crawled toward the enemy. He threw grenades at them and shot at them. He killed several of the Japanese and allowed his platoon time to escape. He died on the field.

Q: Where did the Americans first invade Europe?

A: America entered the war when Japan bombed Pearl Harbor. American troops fought in the South Pacific against the Japanese while the war in Europe was going on. America didn't engage with Hitler and Germany immediately. Instead, in 1943, American troops invaded Sicily in Italy. This invasion was called "Operation Husky." Capturing Sicily gave the Allied forces a way to move ships around the Mediterranean. It also meant that Hitler had to send troops to Italy, weakening his hold in the rest of Europe.

British Lieutenant General Bernard L. Montgomery (left) and US Army Lieutenant General George S. Patton Jr. (right) look over a map of Sicily, circa July–August 1943.

Q: Which British soldier smuggled himself in and out of Auschwitz?

A: Charles Coward was a British soldier captured by the Germans at Calais. He was sent to a labor camp near the Auschwitz concentration camp. Because he could speak German, the Germans put him in charge of the British prisoners of war, which let him move around the labor camp. He often sent coded messages back to Britain, through the Red Cross, about what he witnessed. He smuggled many Jewish prisoners out of Auschwitz by swapping identities with them. In 1943, he traded places with a Jewish prisoner by smuggling himself in and out of Auschwitz to experience the horrors himself. He saved hundreds of Jewish people and was called "the Count of Auschwitz."

Q: How were hedgehogs and mousetraps used in the Battle of the Atlantic?

A: Hedgehogs and mousetraps were special bomb launchers on Allied ships in the Atlantic. The weapons were designed especially to take out German U-boats. The weapons would launch a series of bombs into the water ahead of where the crew believed the U-boat was heading. They only exploded if they actually hit the U-boat, so the sailors could tell exactly where the submarines were. The British first began launching them in 1943. They proved to be very successful, with a kill ratio of 5.7 to one, meaning for every 5.7 uses they succeeded once, which is a very high ratio. In contrast, for example, British depth charges had a kill ratio of 60.5 to one.

Hedgehog bombs

Q: What was the largest Jewish uprising during the war?

A: Hitler's plan to commit genocide against all the Jewish people in Europe had already resulted in a terrible loss of life. In an attempt to defend themselves, the Jewish Combat Organization was formed. On April 19, 1943, the Germans entered the Jewish area (called "the ghetto") of Warsaw, Poland, in a plan to remove all the Jewish people to death camps. The Jewish Combat Organization attacked the Germans with the few weapons and grenades they had available. The Germans lost 12 soldiers and had to retreat. They returned and began burning the buildings in the ghetto to force the Jewish people out. The combat fighters continued to fight. Some held out for over a month. Eventually the entire area, including the Great Synagogue, was burned. More than 100,000 Jews were captured and sent to camps. Although this ended in tragedy, it is remembered as the biggest Jewish uprising in the war and is called the Warsaw Ghetto Uprising.

Q: What change made to German U-boats in 1943 allowed them to stay submerged for longer periods of time?

A: U-boats originally were designed to run on diesel when they were on the surface. When they were submerged, they had to run on batteries because the diesel engines used all the oxygen inside the U-boat. In 1943 they were redesigned with a pipe system called *schnorchel* (which means snorkel) that allowed the diesel engine to run underwater without using all the oxygen in the submarine. They could then stay under the water for a day at a time, making them harder to track.

Q: Why was a wagon full of cats the first vehicle brought into Leningrad when the blockade was broken?

A: The Nazis held the Soviet city of Leningrad under siege for two years, ending in 1943 when a narrow roadway was opened. During the siege, the citizens of Leningrad were starving. They were so hungry they were forced to eat all the cats in the city. Because of this, the rat population exploded. Once the roadway was opened, a wagon full of cats was the first thing brought in, to try to get rid of the rats.

Q: Which German general surrendered the day after his promotion?

A: General Friedrich Paulus commanded the German troops at the Battle of Stalingrad. The Soviets were victorious over the German forces. On January 30, 1943, Hitler promoted Paulus to field marshal to try to give him confidence so he would keep fighting. He ordered him not to surrender. The next day Paulus surrendered to the Soviets. Along with Paulus, 108,000 German troops also surrendered. Only 5,000 of those troops survived until the end of the war (most died on the forced march to Siberia)

Q: What happened to the Japanese man who planned the attack on Pearl Harbor?

A: Japanese admiral Isoroku Yamamoto planned the attack on Pearl Harbor. Although he believed the Japanese would dominate in a war in the Pacific, he predicted they would not win. He believed the Japanese would run out of oil. On April 18, 1943, Yamamoto took a flight to Guadalcanal to visit the troops. American code breakers learned about his travel plan. American forces shot down his plane over the island of Bougainville. This was called

Operation Vengeance. He was found in the wreckage of his plane, upright in his seat with his hand on his sword.

Q: What was Black May?

A: The German navy believed they could win the Battle of the Atlantic by sheer math. Their plan was to sink as many convoys as they could. The convoys carried supplies and troops across the Atlantic. If those men and supplies didn't make it through, the Germans could win the war. The strategy was to use U-boats to sink as many convoys as possible. The Allied forces soon realized that the Germans sunk roughly the same number of ships in each convoy, no matter how big the convoy was. They started making the convoys bigger, so that more ships would get through. This new strategy, combined with improved sonar, meant that the Allies were able to get more ships through while sinking more U-boats. In May 1943 the Allies lost 43 ships but managed to sink 43 U-boats. The Germans called this "Black May" because it showed they could no longer dominate with U-boat attacks. The Germans gave up this strategy.

Q: How did Mussolini escape after being deposed?

A: Benito Mussolini had been Italy's Prime Minister since 1922. He hadn't been doing a very good job during the war and had lost the battle in Africa. On July 9, 1943, Allied planes bombed Rome, damaging its airports. Later that month, members of the Italian government blamed him for doing such a poor job and voted that they had no confidence in him. The king then replaced him with someone else.

Mussolini was arrested and imprisoned in Hotel Campo Imperatore on top of a mountain in the Apennines in southern

Italy. He was guarded by 200 soldiers. Hitler was determined to rescue him. He sent several people to find him and get him out. This was called "the Gran Sasso raid." Soon they discovered where he was being held. The hotel had a flat area next to it, and the Germans determined they could send in a glider plane to land there and get him out.

On September 12, 10 glider planes set out for the hotel from Rome. The area they planned to land on was rockier than they thought, so they had to do a crash landing. While the gliders were landing, paratroopers had landed at the base of the mountain. They took over the funicular (cable car) railway that was the only way to get down the mountain and cut all the phone lines.

The German troops stormed the hotel and broke the guards' radios. The Italian guards surrendered. They found Mussolini who said, "I knew my friend Adolf Hitler wouldn't desert me." A plane came and picked up Mussolini. Mussolini made it out and was reunited with Hitler on September 14. Hitler set him up as the head of a government Hitler declared in charge of Italy, but Mussolini was no longer in charge. Hitler was. Mussolini and his mistress were later captured by the Allies in 1945 when they tried to escape to Switzerland. He was shot by a firing squad.

Q: How were flares used in the Battle of the Ruhr?

A: British forces were sent to bomb the Ruhr region of Germany. This region had many factories that were important to Germany's war effort. Beginning in March 1943, Britain would send Pathfinder Mosquito planes in first. These planes dropped colorful flares over the area that was to be attacked. The flares lit up the exact target, and then bomber planes followed and dropped bombs over the lit-up areas. Each night they bombed a different area, so the Germans had no idea where to position their own planes and anti-aircraft guns.

Q: What were bouncing bombs?

A: In May 1943, British bombers attacked dams on the Möhne and Eder Rivers. The bombs were dropped from a low height so that they skipped across the top of the water. They sank when they got to the walls of the dam and exploded there. The dams held, but power was taken out so that the dams could not function and land all around the dams were flooded.

Q: How did Britain create a firestorm to take out Hamburg?

A: In July 1943 British bombers attacked the German city of Hamburg in Operation Gomorrah. First they dropped bombs that blew out the windows and doors of buildings. Then they dropped firebombs that started fires. They dropped 2,300 tons of bombs in just one day. It was windy and the wind increased the flames. The city was engulfed in a firestorm and 42,000 people died.

Q: What was the *la bataille du rail* (the Battle of the Rails)?

A: As soon as Germany occupied France, many French people worked together to form the French Resistance. This was a network of people who passed messages, smuggled out Allied soldiers who crashed in France, and tried to sabotage everything the Germans were doing. In the summer of 1943, they targeted the railways. Germans used the rail system to move troops and supplies. To protect themselves, the Germans attached civilian rail cars to their trains so that the Allied troops would not bomb them. The resistance fighters found a way to time explosions on the rails so that only the Nazi cars were hit and the civilian cars were undamaged. On the day after D-Day, the resistance fighters cut 3,000 train lines, making it hard for the Nazis to get troops to the beaches. After the war, 200,000 people were honored for their work in the resistance.

Q: Who were the Chindits?

A: The Chindits were a group of British special forces who specialized in long-range penetration. This meant they were sent in by parachute behind Japanese lines and fought in the jungle. The unit was named after a Buddhist statue. The Chindits carried packs that weighed 72 pounds but were heavier when wet. They fought in terrible heat in dense jungle. The first Chindit campaign was fought in Burma in 1943. The Chindits were controversial because although they had an impact, many of them died, were injured, or became ill with tropical diseases. One-third of the Chindits in their first campaign did not make it out. Those who survived were very ill.

Q: How did an American pilot take down a Japanese plane with a pistol?

A: Owen Baggett was a US Army Air Force pilot in the 7th Bomb Group flying a B-24 Liberator over Burma. His mission was to bomb a bridge and destroy it. Baggett and the other pilots in his group ran into Japanese Zero fighters (Mitsubishi A6M planes). The Japanese fired at Baggett's plane and his fuel tanks were hit. Baggett and others had to parachute out of the plane before it exploded.

The Japanese fired at the men as they were parachuting to the ground. Two other men were killed as they hung from their parachutes. Baggett was shot in the arm. He decided to play dead, hoping the Japanese would think they had already killed him. But as he hung from the parachute, he pulled his .45-caliber handgun out of its holster and held it against his leg. At an altitude of 4,000 feet, one of the Japanese fighters flew directly next to Baggett. The Japanese pilot slowed down his plane so much that it almost stalled. He opened the hatch on his plane so he could look at Baggett to see if he was dead.

Baggett was holding his pistol in his hand. He immediately shot four shots at the Japanese pilot. The pilot was shot in the head and died, and his body flew out of the plane. The plane crashed.

Baggett landed safely but was captured by Japanese forces and was held as a POW. Baggett didn't know he'd actually killed the pilot until another soldier who was there that day told him what he'd seen.

Q: What problem did the Americans face as they tried to land at Tarawa?

A: On November 20, 1943, the United States Marines were sent to the island of Betio in the Tarawa Atoll in the Pacific. When they arrived, it was low tide. The marines' boats got stuck on a coral reef and couldn't make it to the shore. The Japanese fired on them as they tried to get the boats through. The marines jumped in the water and waded to the shore through water that came up to their chests. Most of their equipment, including radios, got wet and was unusable. They fought for more than three days before taking control of the island.

Q: What unusual request did US General Dwight Eisenhower make in 1943?

A: On June 29, 1943, General Eisenhower sent a cablegram from his headquarters in North Africa to the Coca-Cola headquarters. The general wanted Coca-Cola to send 3 million bottles of soda. He also wanted the company to send the equipment and materials needed to build 10 bottling plants in North Africa so that the soda could be produced on site for the troops. Six months later, the first Coca-Cola plant opened in Algiers. All together, 64 Coca-Cola bottling plants were built overseas close to the fronts to supply the troops during the war. More than 5 billion bottles of Coke were drunk by servicemen during the war.

Q: What was the smallest army that fought in World War II?

A: The Greenland army had only 15 men. The Germans tried several times to take control of different areas of Greenland. Establishing control of Greenland would have given the Germans the ability to see the weather that was developing. The weather in Europe comes from the Arctic, so being able to see storms forming and predict how they would impact Europe would have helped the Germans. The Germans landed on Greenland's Sabine Island in 1943. Greenlanders noticed them. The governor of the area was worried the Germans might try to wage war with the 15 Greenlanders in the area. If they were captured, they would be considered bandits by the Nazis and executed. So he declared that they were the Greenland army. If captured, they would have to be treated like POWs. This small army did end up fighting the Germans. One was killed. Two were captured though they managed not only to escape but also to capture one of the Germans. Allied bombers took out the weather station the Germans had been setting up.

Q: Which US ship was actually a British ship?

A: When the USS *Hornet* was lost in 1942, it left the American navy with only one fleet carrier, the USS *Saratoga*. The Americans needed another ship and didn't have time to wait for one to be built. The British ship HMS *Victorious* was loaned to the Americans in 1943. The ship was repainted with American colors and given an ice cream parlor and a Coca-Cola machine. The crew put on American uniforms. The ship was renamed the USS *Robin*. The British called it "the Limey flat top." The ship served in the Pacific. By July of 1943, the Americans had new aircraft carriers and the HMS *Victorious* was returned to the British.

Q: Which German pilot escorted a wounded American pilot to safety?

A: On December 20, 1943, American lieutenant Charlie Brown was the commander of a B-17 on a bombing run over Germany. His plane was severely damaged and he was shot in the shoulder. He lost consciousness and woke up just before the plane crashed and got it back up in the air. German Luftwaffe pilot Franz Stigler saw that no one was manning the guns of the plane and how badly the plane was damaged. He knew the men inside were seriously hurt. He pulled up next to it in the air and saw Brown. He tried to signal to him that he would help him but Brown didn't understand. Stigler escorted the plane all the way across open water until he was sure it could get back to Britain safely. He saluted and flew away. Years later Brown and Stigler found each other and became friends.

Q: How did an American ship take down a Japanese sub using potatoes?

A: In 1943, the USS *O'Bannon* had finished fighting in the Solomon Islands in the Pacific and was on its way back to its station at night. It sailed close to the Japanese submarine *RO-34*. The sub was on the surface and the Japanese sailors were sleeping on top of it. Because of a fear of possible mines in the area, the *O'Bannon* ended up steering itself right next to the sub. The Japanese woke up and scrambled to get to their deck guns. The *O'Bannon* was so close to the sub that the Americans could not use any of their deck guns or other weapons to fire at the sub. The ship did have boxes of potatoes on the deck, and the Americans grabbed them and started throwing them at the Japanese. The Japanese assumed they were grenades and ran around trying to grab them and throw them back at the *O'Bannon*. This gave the *O'Bannon* enough time to move back so it could fire at the sub. The sub was sunk thanks to potatoes.

USS *O'Bannon*

Q: How did an American convince 1,500 Japanese to surrender?

A: Corporal Guy Gabaldon was a Mexican American raised by a Japanese family in the United States. He joined the marines and was sent to Saipan in 1943. On his first night, he went out alone and talked two Japanese soldiers into surrendering. His superiors warned him not to go out alone again, but he didn't listen. He went back out and encountered 50 Japanese soldiers in a cave. He killed their guard and shouted into the cave that they were surrounded and if they came out they would not kill them. They listened to him and surrendered. His superiors saw his talents and sent him again. This time he brought in 800 Japanese soldiers. During the Battle of Tinian he was able to convince 1,500 Japanese soldiers and civilians to surrender in the area. He received the Navy Cross for his work.

Q: What role did Dr. Seuss play in the war?

A: American citizen Theodor Geisel (known as Dr. Seuss) was an editorial cartoonist before the war. He enlisted in 1943. The army sent him to Fox Studios (called "Fort Fox") in California to work in Frank Capra's signal corps in the animation department of the First Motion Picture Unit. This group created training manuals and films used to teach soldiers. Geisel worked on a series of humorous, short animated films about Private Snafu (which stands for "Situation Normal All Fouled Up"), a soldier who made all the mistakes that soldiers should not make. He included some of his rhymes in these films, such as "The moral, Snafu, is that the harder you work, the sooner we're gonna beat Hitler, that jerk." He flew to Europe to show the films to army generals and was trapped behind enemy lines for 10 days during the Battle of the Bulge. He stayed in the army until 1946. After he left, he began writing his famous children's books.

1944

The Allies lost an attempt to take control of the Netherlands. However, the Allied invasion of Normandy (D-Day) was hugely successful and was a major turning point in the war. The siege of Leningrad was broken. The Battle of the Bulge was begun. Poland was liberated from Nazi control. In the Pacific, the Americans were victorious at Leyte Gulf in the Philippines and in Guam.

Q: What musical instrument was played on the beach during the invasion of Normandy?

A: The bagpipes. Bill Millin was a member of the British 1st Special Service Brigade that landed at Sword Beach on June 6, 1944, in France. Millin had brought his bagpipes along, and his commander asked him to play them on the beach during the invasion to keep spirits up. Although it was against the rules to do this, Millin played songs like "Highland Laddie" and "Road to the Isles." He later found out the Germans occupying France did not shoot at him because they thought he was crazy. Once the troops moved inland, his commander asked him to play again as they crossed a bridge.

Bill Millin playing his bagpipes

Q: How did stealth mules help win the war?

A: The battles in Burma (which is called "Myanmar" today) were fought between the Allied forces and the Japanese. Burma was filled with mountains and rivers, and it was difficult for vehicles to get in to bring supplies to the troops. Donkeys or mules worked well to carry in supplies. The only problem, though, was that the

WWII BATTLE TRIVIA FOR KIDS

donkeys would bray and alert the enemy as to the location of the troops. The solution was that the donkeys had surgery to silence their vocal cords so they could be stealthy. Because so many donkeys were needed, many were flown in and dropped out of planes with parachutes.

Q: What was the first ship sunk by a kamikaze pilot?

A: On October 25, 1994, the USS *St. Lo* was the first major warship sunk by a kamikaze. Because they were unable to defend themselves against the Allied naval forces during the Battle of Leyte Gulf, the Japanese needed a new strategy. They decided to fill planes with explosives and send pilots to fly them directly into their targets. They called them "kamikaze," which means "divine wind" in Japanese. The pilots proudly took on the missions, believing that it was an honor to die for their country. Japan flew 2,800 kamikaze missions in the war, sinking 34 US Navy ships, and killing 4,900 members of the navy.

USS *St. Lo* hit by kamikazes

Q: Which Black nurse defied orders and treated white soldiers?

A: Augusta Chiwy, a Belgian Black nurse, didn't plan to volunteer in the war. She was a hospital nurse visiting her family in Bastogne, Belgium, in late 1944. An American doctor knocked on the door and asked for help treating soldiers in the Battle of the Bulge. Chiwy volunteered. More than 80,000 American soldiers were killed, wounded, or captured in the battle. There was just one doctor to treat them. Army regulations said that a Black nurse could not treat white soldiers, but Dr. John Prior told the men they had a choice between dying and being treated by her. Chiwy also often went outside the hospital onto the battlefield under fire to look for wounded men to treat. At one point she was covered in blood and put on an army uniform since she had nothing else. A civilian putting on the uniform was punishable by death at that time. She received several awards and medals for her service.

Q: Who were the Aztec Eagles?

A: Although Mexico technically joined in the war, it was not an active participant. Mexico supplied materials to support the war, but did not send troops. That is, until 1945. The president of Mexico wanted a more active role so he sent an air force squadron called the Aztec Eagles to the US for training. The squadron had 33 pilots as well as support staff. The squadron was sent to the Philippines where it flew missions and dropped bombs in the south Pacific. Mexico also allowed the US government to force Mexican citizens in the US to enlist in the military. Fifteen thousand Mexican citizens were drafted.

Q: What was the Lost Battalion?

A: The American 1st Battalion of the 141st Infantry Regiment from Texas was in the Vosges Mountains in France in October of 1944. There were 275 men in the unit. They were surrounded by the Germans and completely cut off from the rest of the American troops and lost contact. They were running out of food and water despite some airdropped supplies. Hitler ordered that the unit should be prevented from being rescued no matter what.

The 100th/442nd Regimental Combat Team was sent to rescue them. This segregated unit was made up of second-generation Japanese American soldiers (called "nisei") who were finally allowed to serve after many Japanese Americans were held in internment camps because they were believed to be possible enemies.

Six days after the Lost Battalion was trapped, the nisei moved in and battled with the Germans for five days. They were outnumbered four to one and frequently fought in hand-to-hand combat, often in mud. The nisei finally reached the battalion and received a Presidential Unit Citation for their bravery. Two hundred and eleven members of the Lost Battalion were brought out alive because of their courage

Q: How was the USS *Tang* sunk?

A: The USS *Tang* was a Balao-class American submarine. She was launched from Pearl Harbor in 1944. *Tang* was the most successful American submarine with 33 confirmed kills. Later that year, she launched a torpedo at a Japanese tanker ship. The torpedo turned and followed a circular pattern and ended up hitting the *Tang* itself. The submarine was sunk and 78 men were lost.

Q: What was a pillbox and how did one play a role in the taking of Cherbourg?

A: After the US forces landed at Utah Beach in June 1944, they slowly worked their way inland. The goal was to take the Contentin peninsula and the city of Cherbourg from the Germans. The Germans lost ground but held their position in Fort du Roule in the hills. The Americans

A World War II–era pillbox

approached but could not get close because of constant fire from a pillbox. A pillbox is a stone or cement guardhouse with holes for guns to fire through. Corporal John D. Kelly crawled forward while under fire. He carried a 10-foot stick with TNT at the end. He lit the charge, but it didn't go off. He crawled back to safety and got another. He crawled back to the pillbox and dropped it down a periscope hole. The smoke forced the Germans out and Americans were able to take the fort. Kelly died later that year. He was awarded a Medal of Honor after his death.

Q: What was the only country in South America to fight in World War II?

A: In 1942, Brazil became the only South American country to declare war against Germany. Brazilian troops were deployed in 1944 in Europe. Brazilian pilots flew 445 missions. The Brazilian Expeditionary Force had 100,000 soldiers. At that time there was a saying in Brazil: "when snakes smoke." This was similar to the expression "when pigs fly," meaning something that will never happen. Before Brazil entered the war, people said they would become involved when snakes smoked. Because they did enter

the war, their soldiers called themselves "the Smoking Snakes."
They wore a patch on their uniforms of a snake smoking a pipe.

Q: Did German and American soldiers ever celebrate Christmas together during the war?

A: On December 24, 1944, during the Battle of the Bulge, Elisabeth Vincken, a German, was alone with her son in a cabin in the woods. Three American soldiers were lost and came upon the cabin. One of them was wounded. They knocked on her door and she let them in and shared what little food she had with them. While they were eating, German soldiers also came to her door. They were also lost and hungry. Harboring enemy soldiers was punished with death so she was afraid, but admitted to them there were Americans inside. She told them there was not going to be any shooting on Christmas Eve. She had the Germans leave their weapons outside. They all ate together. One of the Germans was a medical student who helped the wounded American. They started to talk. When they parted ways in the morning, the Germans gave the Americans directions back to their troops and gave them a compass. They all shook hands and said good-bye.

Q: Which Black Panther defied orders and continued to fight despite a serious wound?

A: Platoon Sergeant Ruben Rivers was a Black and Cherokee American who fought with the 761st Tank Battalion. This all–African American battalion was called "the Black Panthers." On November 16, 1944, Rivers commanded his battalion of Sherman tanks as they attacked the German town of Guebling. His tank went over a land mine and flipped over. His leg was wounded and open to the bone. With this injury he could have survived and been sent home. Instead, he refused treatment and insisted on continuing to fight. The next two days he continued to fight, driving tanks even though he developed gangrene. He died when his tank was blown up by German fire.

Q: How did a silver dollar save a future senator's life?

A: Daniel Inouye was a second-generation Japanese American who lived in Honolulu. When he was a teenager, curfews were enforced for Japanese Americans on the island, and there was talk of sending the people of Japanese descent to internment camps. These were set up in California to imprison Japanese Americans the government considered enemies. Japanese Americans were not allowed to enlist until 1943 when they were permitted to join segregated units of Japanese Americans called "nisei." Inouye enlisted and became a member of the 442nd Regimental Combat Team.

Inouye was in the Vosges Mountains in France when his unit was sent to rescue what was called "the Lost Battalion." (See page 109.) Inouye was shot in the chest by the Germans. However, he was not wounded because he had silver dollar coins in the pocket of his shirt. He decided the coins were good luck charms and kept them with him after that.

Later that year, he was sent to Italy. One day he realized he had lost his lucky silver dollars. That same day he was shot by the Germans. He continued throwing grenades even though he was wounded. He went to throw another grenade, and as he was pulling his arm back, a German shot him in the arm. He pulled the grenade out of his wounded hand and threw it with his other hand. He kept moving forward and shooting at the Germans until he was shot again and passed out. He survived, but he had to have his arm amputated. Inouye was awarded the Distinguished Service Cross and later, the Medal of Honor. Inouye went on to become one of Hawaii's senators and was the first Japanese American to serve in Congress.

Senator Daniel K. Inouye receives the Medal of Honor flag.

Q: How did a female war correspondent get to the front lines for D-Day?

A: Martha Gellhorn was a war correspondent in London for *Collier's*. No women were being sent to the front lines to report. Her husband, writer Ernest Hemingway, was allowed to go. Martha didn't believe this was fair. She snuck onto a hospital ship headed to France and stowed away on it. She locked herself in a bathroom so she wouldn't be discovered. She managed to be the only woman on the beaches at Normandy in the days following D-Day. She went ashore and helped bring wounded men back to the ship.

Q: What were strongholds and why did Hitler order them?

A: On March 9, 1944, Hitler issued an order creating strongholds along the Eastern front where Germany was fighting the Soviets. A stronghold was a place that he said had to be held at all costs. A stronghold city had to allow itself to be completely encircled by the Soviets, but keep fighting no matter what. Although he knew most of these towns and cities could not be defended forever, he knew that trying to do so would keep the Soviet troops busy. The Soviets would not be able to fight anywhere else. He knew that he would lose many soldiers but didn't care.

Q: Why where there no marines on the beach at D-Day?

A: The Marine Corps is specially trained in amphibious war, so it would make sense to use them at D-Day. However no marines were on shore during the invasion. The reason goes back to World War I. After the World War I Battle of Belleau Wood, American newspapers gave credit for the victory to the marines and made little mention of the army. This created a rivalry between the two forces. The army leaders planning the D-Day invasion were determined that the marines would not get the credit for the victory they hoped for. Marines were present at sea that day and provided lookouts and other supportive roles. The night before the invasion, General Patton talked to his troops and told them that the quicker they could get the job done, the quicker they could go face the Japanese and beat them before the marines "`get all the credit."

Q: What type of boat was key to the Americans landing on D-Day?

A: The LCVP (landing craft, vehicle, personnel) or Higgins boat was what made D-Day possible. It was a small, shallow boat with a bow that opened so troops could run out. Each boat held 36 men or 6,000 pounds of vehicles and equipment. Four crew members were needed to operate each boat. The boats could go 12 knots and were fitted with machine guns. General Eisenhower said that without them "We never could have landed over an open beach. The whole strategy of the war would have been different." The

Americans manufactured 23,000 of the boats during the war, and they were used in both the Atlantic and Pacific.

An LCVP being employed on D-Day

Q: What machine helped the Allied forces choose the best time for D-Day?

A: The Allies wanted to land at Normandy as a low tide was ending so that they could send forces in to remove barriers the Germans had placed in the water. They then wanted to bring the rest of the troops ashore at a high tide, so there would be less beach for them to cross under enemy fire. They also wanted to cross the Atlantic in the dark and begin landing in the daylight. To determine when all of these factors could align, a British oceanographer named Arthur Doodson used a tidal predictor machine. The machine helped determine when the low and high tides would be on specific days and helped the Allies plan their invasion at the best possible time.

Q: What was the Red Ball Express?

A: After the Allies took the beaches in Normandy, they needed supplies as they continued to fight. The Allies destroyed the French railroad system to stop the Germans from using it. Each combat division needed 750 tons of supplies per day. The Allies needed a way to get the supplies through. They created what was called "the Red Ball Express." The Allies drove trucks with big red dots on their roofs along highways. The red dots were to let the airborne Allied forces know the trucks were their own so they didn't bomb them. Over 6,000 trucks carried 12,000 tons of needed supplies each day.

Q: How did an assassination attempt on Hitler's life almost end the war?

A: In July 1944 many of Hitler's team had lost hope. They were sure Germany was going to lose the war. They wanted to end Hitler's rule. Claus von Stauffenberg and two other men planned an assassination. They were going to use Hitler's death to create a new government. The new government would end the war. They called the plan "Operation Valkyrie."

Stauffenberg knew Hitler was going to have a meeting at what was called "the Wolf's Lair" on July 20. This was a concrete, secret bunker. The bunker was underground with a steel door. Stauffenberg planned to bring a bomb into the bunker. The plan was the bomb would be sealed in the room with Hitler and it would kill everyone inside. However, that day was hot so the meeting was moved to a wooden building upstairs that had windows.

Stauffenberg brought a bomb into the room in a suitcase. He sat as close to Hitler as he could and put the suitcase on the

WWII BATTLE TRIVIA FOR KIDS

floor. He pretended he needed to make a phone call and got up and left the room. While he was gone, someone moved the suitcase behind a heavy table leg. He detonated the bomb but because the meeting was in a wooden building and the bomb was behind a heavy table leg, Hitler was not killed. One person died and 20 were injured. Stauffenberg fled but was captured and executed.

Q: What was Big Week?

A: The Allies planned a weeklong air attack against Germany. The week of February 19, 1944, the Allied air forces began bombing German airplane factories. This drew the Luftwaffe into an air battle. During this week, the Luftwaffe lost 18 percent of its pilots and a third of its planes. By weakening the Luftwaffe, the Allied forces had set the stage for D-Day.

Q: What was the American response when the Germans demanded they surrender at Bastogne?

A: The American 101st Airborne Division was cornered in the Belgium city of Bastogne on December 18, 1944. They were running out of food and ammunition. Although it was winter, they didn't have cold-weather gear. They were outnumbered five to one by Germans. When the Germans demanded they surrender on December 22, Brigadier General Anthony McAuliffe sent back a one-word response: "Nuts." Supplies were soon airdropped and General Patton arrived on December 26, taking the city and pushing the Germans back.

Q: What was the British Fourth Army?

A: The British Fourth Army was a fake army the British set up in Scotland. It was made up to fool the Germans while the Allies planned the invasion at Normandy. The British pretended the Fourth Army was getting ready to invade Norway. This drew German forces away from France so that the Allies could take Normandy.

Q: How many Allied troops died on D-Day?

A: On June 6, 1944, the Allied troops stormed the beaches at Normandy. A total of 150,000 Allied troops made the attack. Only 9,000 died, far less than Allied command anticipated.

Q: Which countries stormed which beaches at Normandy?

A: Allied command broke the Normandy beaches up into five different areas. Each area was invaded by one country's forces:

- Sword Beach (Britain)
- Juno Beach (Canada)
- Gold Beach (Britain)
- Omaha Beach (United States)
- Utah Beach (United States)

Although they attacked on different beaches, the operation was carefully coordinated. The Americans went first, then the British, then the Canadians.

Q: What was the name of the Allied operation for D-Day?

A: The plan to invade Normandy, France, for D-Day was called "Operation Overlord."

Q: What happened at Bloody Nose Ridge?

A: In September of 1944, American troops moved to take control of the Palau Islands in the Pacific. Peleliu was the target. They bombed the area and then sent in troops by sea. The troops were sent in waves until there were enough to move onto the island. The Japanese had seen this tactic before and used a strategy called "attrition." This meant they planned to hold their ground and just continue to fight. The Japanese hid in caves and on cliffs above the Americans. The Americans called this area "Bloody Nose Ridge." The eight-day battle caused the Americans to lose half of their men (more than 9,000 troops). Eventually more troops arrived and the Americans were able to surround the Japanese. The Japanese held to their strategy and did not give up. Nearly all of them were killed.

Q: Who were the first Black American troops to participate in combat in the war?

A: On June 15, 1944, American troops landed on the beach of Saipan in the Pacific. Among them were 800 Black marines who unloaded all of the supplies and ammunition. They moved all of these items to the troops on the beach while under fire from the Japanese.

Q: Who was the highest-ranking American killed in the war?

A: Lieutenant General Lesley J. McNair was the highest-ranking American killed in World War II. On July 25, 1944, McNair was visiting troops in France. He was killed by an Allied bomb in a friendly fire incident. McNair is also known for serving while suffering from a severe hearing loss. A waiver was issued that allowed him to continue to serve despite this.

Q: Which relative of Hitler convinced the US president to let him serve in the navy?

A: William Patrick Hitler was the son of Hitler's half-brother Alois Hitler and was Hitler's half-nephew. William was born and raised in England and lived in Germany for a time as an adult. He met his Uncle Adolph a few times. He began giving lectures about what he knew about his uncle. William was visiting the United States when the US joined the war. He tried to join the US military but was denied because of his name. He wrote a letter to President Roosevelt asking to be allowed to serve. Roosevelt agreed. He was cleared by the FBI. William served in the navy as a pharmacist's mate from 1944 to 1947. He later changed his last name to Stuart-Houston.

Q: How did a Korean man end up being captured at Normandy on D-Day?

A: Yang Kyoungjong was a Korean man who was conscripted into the Japanese army when Japan invaded China. Soviet forces fought with Japanese forces on the Chinese-Soviet border. Jong was captured by the Soviets and conscripted into their army. When Germany invaded the Soviet Union, Jong was captured by Germans and conscripted again, this time into their army. Jong was sent with German troops to Normandy where he wore a German uniform and was captured by Americans on D-Day.

Q: Which soldier refused to accept a Distinguished Conduct Medal?

A: Canadian soldier Léo Major was at the Battle of the Scheldt in 1944 when he was sent out to find a group of new soldiers who had been lost while on patrol. It was wet and cold. He came across two

German soldiers and said to himself that it was because of them that he was wet and cold and so they would pay. He captured one German and then killed the other. He captured their commanding officer, who surrendered the entire group. He began to escort them back as prisoners. Another group of German soldiers saw this and shot at their own soldiers, killing several. Major kept marching the rest. He came up to a Canadian tank and ordered it to fire on the Germans who were firing at him. He ended up bringing back 100 prisoners. Major also acted bravely in 1945. He and another soldier were sent to scout the Dutch city of Zwolle, which was controlled by Germans. His companion was killed. Major went through the city, firing guns and setting fires. The Germans believed they had been attacked by an entire group of Allied soldiers. The Germans fled and the Allies were able to retake the town. He was supposed to be awarded a Distinguished Conduct Medal. He refused because he said the general who was going to give it to him was incompetent.

Q: Which airman flew his plane underneath the Eiffel Tower?

A: American fighter pilot William Overstreet Jr. was a member of the 357th Fighter Group escorting American bombers above Nazi-occupied France in 1944. A dogfight began with the Germans and Overstreet followed a German plane. He pursued the

William Overstreet Jr.

German plane through the streets of Paris and then under the Eiffel Tower. After this, he shot down the German plane.

Q: Which spy received both British and German medals?

A: Juan Pujol García was a Spanish citizen who wanted to help the Allies. He applied to be a spy for the British and was rejected. He then created a false identity and became a German agent who made up all the reports he gave the Germans. The British were impressed and took him on as a spy. He continued to act as a double agent, loyal to Britain. In 1944 the Germans awarded him the Iron Cross because they thought he had done a good job. The British awarded him the Member of the British Empire medal for his work that same year.

Q: What was the American Ghost Army?

A: In 1944 and 1945 members of the American 23rd Headquarters Special Troops were sent to Europe to fool the Germans. A group of 1,100 troops were sent to pretend to be a real army. They set up areas near the front lines and displayed inflatable tanks and rubber airplanes to convince the Germans the Americans had more resources than they actually did. The members pretended to be members of other units by sewing their identification onto their uniforms. They went and sat at French restaurants and talked about made-up operations. Engineers also recorded battle sounds and then played them loud enough so they could be heard miles away, making the Germans think there was action nearby. They also had spoof radio communications. Actors pretended to be radio operators who sent Morse code communications. They convinced the Germans that troops who were no longer nearby were still in the area.

Q: Who saved Paris from total destruction by the Nazis?

A: German general Dietrich von Choltitz was the last German commander in Paris. At the time he was placed in control, the Allied forces were closing in. His orders from Hitler were to destroy important bridges and buildings instead of letting them fall into Allied control. He disobeyed this order. Instead, he negotiated a truce and returned control of Paris to the Allies on August 25, 1944.

Q: What were paradummies?

A: During the D-Day landings, the Allies launched thousands of dolls that looked like paratroopers from planes, with parachutes. The goal was to trick the Germans into thinking they were deploying troops in other areas. Many of the paradummies exploded when they hit the ground so that the Germans would think they had been shot at. They also dropped actual soldiers alongside them who played battle recordings so it sounded real.

Q: Which rocket launched during the war was the first object to reach space?

A: The Germans developed the V-2 rocket (called Aggregat 4) and launched it in 1944. It was the first long-range ballistic missile and the very first man-made object to go high enough to reach what is considered space because it passed what is called "the Kármán line," the boundary between Earth's atmosphere and outer space. It had a 200-mile range and carried a one-ton warhead.

Aggregat 4

Q: Who received a Bronze Star for a prayer?

A: On April 8, 1944, General Patton's army was in France during the Battle of the Bulge. It had been raining, and the Allies needed dry weather to advance. General Patton asked Chaplain James O'Neill to pray for good weather. O'Neill typed up the following:

"Almighty and most merciful Father, we humbly beseech Thee, of Thy great goodness, to restrain these immoderate rains with which we have had to contend. Grant us fair weather for Battle. Graciously hearken to us as soldiers who call upon Thee that, armed with Thy power, we may advance from victory to victory and crush the oppression and wickedness of our enemies, and establish Thy justice among men and nations. Amen."

Patton ordered that 250,000 copies be distributed. The weather did eventually clear and Patton gave O'Neill a Bronze Star.

1945

The final year of the war was 1945. The Battle of the Bulge ended and Germany was forced to retreat. The last bomb of the war fell on Britain. Hitler committed suicide and Germany surrendered, ending the war in Europe. In the Pacific, the Allies won against the Japanese at Iwo Jima. They then took Okinawa, the last island the Japanese had control of. The Japanese refused to surrender and the United States dropped two atomic bombs on Japan. Japan then surrendered and the war was finally over.

Q: What was the name of the plane that dropped the atomic bomb on Nagasaki, Japan?

A: The first atomic bomb ever (named "Little Boy") was dropped on Hiroshima by the Americans on August 6, 1945, by a plane named *Enola Gay*. The second atomic bomb was dropped on Nagasaki, Japan, on August 9, 1945. The B-29

Bockscar carrying Fat Man

bomber plane carrying that bomb was *Bockscar*, named after its commander, Frederick Bock. The bomb was called "Fat Man." More than 60,000 Japanese were killed by the bomb that day. A third bomb was ready to be dropped a week later, but the Japanese surrendered, ending the war.

Q: Which American fought off over 100 Japanese soldiers?

American private John R. McKinney was alone in his tent in Luzon in the Philippines during the campaign to retake the area. Suddenly, a Japanese soldier slashed his tent, cutting off his ear. Private McKinney fought alone against more than 100 Japanese soldiers who tried to take over his machine gun. Using his rifle and his hands, this hero killed 40 Japanese and held them off from taking over American space. He was awarded the Medal of Honor for his bravery.

Q: How did a toilet lead to the capture of a U-boat crew?

A: In April 1945, *U-1206*, a German U-boat, was off the coast of Scotland. The sub's latrine, or toilet, backed up and filled the air with gas. The U-boat had to surface to let out the gas. Although the German crew tried to escape in rubber rafts, they were captured by the British and their sub sank.

Q: Which country used the largest battalion of flamethrower tanks in the war?

A: While several countries had flamethrower tanks, the US military had an entire battalion of flamethrower tanks at the Battle of Okinawa in 1945. Flamethrower tanks were only effective from a distance of around 33 yards. However, Japanese soldiers were terrified of them because of the terrible fires they could create. Marines developed a method they called "corkscrew and blowtorch" using them. First, they would shoot at bunkers with rifles, cracking them open. Then they would shoot flames into the cracks, setting the entire area on fire.

Flamethrower tank

Q: What did American naval ships fly to celebrate the end of the war?

A: Navy ships flew what were called "homeward bound pennants" to celebrate victory. These colorful fabric flags were so long they sometimes had to be held up by balloons to keep them from hanging into the water. The pennants had a blue background with white stars on the first third. The last two-thirds were covered in red and white stripes. It ended in a swallowtail. The pennants were flown by ships that had been in battle for at least 12 months. They were flown on the final voyage from their last port until they were home. When the ship reached her home port, the pennant was brought down and cut into pieces. Each sailor was given a piece to commemorate their victory.

Q: Which hospital ship was hit by a kamikaze attack?

A: Hospital ships were used as active combat care units during the war. Wounded and injured servicemen were immediately treated on the ships. The ships were protected by the Geneva and Hague Conventions, international treaties that lay out the rules for war. Hospital ships were painted white with a red cross and had to leave their lights on at all times, even if they were with a convoy of military ships. The USS *Comfort* was hit by a kamikaze attack on April 28, 1945. Seventeen people in the surgery unit were killed.

Q: How did the USO celebrate VJ Day?

A: On August 15, 1945, Japan surrendered, ending World War II. The surrender created a lot of emotion as people danced in the streets, cried, and hugged. In Naples, Italy, a famous singing group called the Andrews Sisters was performing for the USO in front of a huge crowd of soldiers. Patty Andrews announced the surrender.

There was dead silence. She announced it again and said it was true and began to cry. The entire crowd roared. In Honolulu, the USO club always served food to servicemen but sold it at cost. On VJ Day, the club served free food to 12,000 servicemen.

Q: Which ship did the Japanese formally surrender on?

A: On September 2, 1945, the Allied leaders accepted Japan's formal surrender, officially ending the war. To formally surrender, the military leaders met and signed a document with the terms of the surrender. The ceremony was held on the USS *Missouri*. The ship was named after President Truman's home state. His daughter had christened the ship. The ship had been in battle at Okinawa and Iwo Jima. B-29 Superfortresses flew overhead during the ceremony. After the signing, General MacArthur said, "Today the guns are silent. A great tragedy has ended. A great victory has been won. The skies no longer rain death, the seas bear only commerce, men everywhere walk upright in the sunlight. The entire world lies quietly at peace. The holy mission has been completed. We have had our last chance. If we do not devise some greater and more equitable system, Armageddon will be at our door."

Q: How did the US Navy use a typhoon to help them take out Japanese ships?

A: The US Navy needed to make headway against Japanese ships. They waited for a typhoon to pass, and then on July 22, 1945, sent nine destroyer ships in at night behind it into Sagami Bay. This was an important area since it was the opening to Tokyo Bay. The ships traveled in a line behind each other. Soon they saw Japanese ships on their radar. All together the nine destroyers launched torpedoes and began firing. They sunk two Japanese ships and then turned and headed to safety.

Q: For which battle were the most Medals of Honor issued?

A: The most Medals of Honor were issued for Iwo Jima in 1945. Twenty-seven of those medals were awarded for bravery in that difficult operation.

Q: Which German general tried to surrender and then committed suicide?

A: Heinrich Himmler was the Reich Commissar for the Strengthening of the German Ethnic Stock. He implemented the concentration camp system and is responsible for the murder of 2.7 million Jewish people and other prisoners during the war. After an assassination attempt against Hitler failed in 1944, Himmler tried to negotiate a surrender to the Allies. He continued to try in 1945, asking the Red Cross to carry his offer of surrender to General Eisenhower. Hitler found out and had him arrested. Himmler escaped by using stolen identity papers, wearing a stolen uniform, and shaving off his mustache. He was captured by the Soviets and turned over to the British. He committed suicide using a cyanide capsule.

Q: How did a leper help the Americans win the Battle of Manila?

A: Josefina Guerrero was a Filipino citizen diagnosed with leprosy (also called Hansen's Disease). The contagious disease causes large skin lesions (sores). Once the Japanese occupied the Philippines, she could not get medication to control it. She decided to work as a spy against the Japanese. Japanese troops searched any Filipino who was moving around, but the soldiers were afraid to come near her because they didn't want to catch leprosy. They didn't search her and she was able to carry messages. In January 1945 she was asked to carry a map of the minefields around Manila to the American headquarters. She taped the map to her back and walked more than 30 miles and was chased by pirates while on a boat. She got the map to the Americans and the troops were able to avoid the mines and win the Battle of Manila.

Q: Which brand of pen was used by both General Eisenhower and General MacArthur at VJ Day and VE Day surrender ceremonies?

A: On May 7, 1945, General Dwight D. Eisenhower formally signed the surrender agreement with German general Alfred Jodl on VE Day. On September 2 of that same year, General Douglas MacArthur formally signed the surrender agreement with Japan on VJ Day. Both men used Parker fountain pens. Eisenhower used a 1945 Parker 51 pen. MacArthur used a 1928 Parker Duofold pen.

Q: How did a treacle factory stop a British tank?

A: In April 1945, the British shelled a treacle factory in Italy. Treacle is a sticky syrup used in Europe. The shells damaged the tanks of treacle and it leaked out. The plant was also bombed and this left big craters. Some of the treacle filled one of the craters. When the British drove their tanks, one got stuck in a crater full of treacle. The soldiers inside had to get out quickly to avoid suffocating. The tank was never rescued.

Q: What was the Prague uprising?

A: Czechoslovakia was occupied by the Germans. On May 5, 1945, the Czech people in Prague decided to take back their city. Czech police officers stormed a radio station and fought with the Germans holding it. The radio broadcasters started calling for everyone in the city to take over the city. People flooded the streets. They took down Nazi flags and flew the Czech flag. They put up 1,600 barriers. Public transport stopped allowing German money.

The people took over most of the city including bridges and train stations. The Germans began bombing the city the next day. Soviet troops arrived and assisted the Czechs. The Germans eventually agreed to a truce.

Q: Which American war correspondent was killed on the field?

A: Journalist Ernie Pyle began covering the war in 1940. He traveled across Europe and the Pacific, writing eyewitness accounts of what the war was like on the front lines. He often mentioned specific units by name, which thrilled the soldiers and helped their family at home to stay informed. He was awarded a Pulitzer Prize for his coverage. He watched the D-Day invasion on D-Day from the bridge of General Omar Bradley's ship. In April 1945 he went ashore with troops on an island near Okinawa. He was in a Jeep with an army officer when a Japanese soldier opened fire. He dove into a ditch, but when he popped his head up to look, he was shot in the head below his helmet and died.

Q: How was napalm used in the invasion of Okinawa?

A: In the very difficult fight at Okinawa in May 1945, the US Marines struggled to overcome the Japanese at Wana Ridge, a valley surrounded by high cliffs. The Japanese hid in caves that the Americans didn't know how to access. The Japanese would enter them via secret tunnels at night. The marines tried to get the Japanese out using various techniques. They soon decided to use napalm, a chemical that easily can be set on fire. The marines carried barrels of napalm up to the tops of the ridges. They used axes and the butts of their rifles to open the barrels. Then they rolled the open barrels down the hills towards the Japanese. Next, they set the trail of napalm on fire using grenades. This killed many Japanese and got the rest to abandon the caves.

Q: What happened to German U-boats at the end of the war?

A: When the Germans surrendered, 156 U-boats were given up to the Allied forces. However, 221 U-boats refused to give in, and their captains scuttled them so that the Allies could not have them.

Q: Which American president and commander in chief died in office shortly before the end of the war?

A: President Franklin D. Roosevelt died on April 12, 1945, just months before the end of the war. He served four terms as president. Harry Truman took over as president and commander in chief and supervised the surrender of the Germans and Japanese later that year.

Q: Which Rhine bridge miraculously survived detonation attempts by the Germans?

A: The Rhine River in Germany is deep, long, and fast. The Allies needed to cross it to get to Ruhr in March 1945. They couldn't ford the river. Germany had blown up most of the bridges that crossed the river.

Ludendorff Bridge

The Ludendorff Bridge in Remagen was left standing, but it was a railway bridge with high ridges at either end. The Germans didn't expect the Allies to attempt a crossing there. Just in case though, they rigged it with explosives. American troops approached the bridge and the Germans set off an explosion, but it didn't damage the bridge because the explosives hadn't been set up properly. The Americans rushed across the bridge. The Germans set off another explosive and the bridge lifted up in the air but settled back in position. The Americans were able to use the bridge for ten days, bringing troops and tanks across it. The bridge finally collapsed on March 17.

Q: How were four American pilots killed after the war had ended?

A: On August 9, 1945, Japanese emperor Hirohito began negotiating Japan's surrender in the war. On August 15, Hirohito went on television in Japan to announce the surrender. Although the surrender was announced, there was one last dogfight (air battle) yet to happen.

Four American pilots, Billy Hobbs, Eugene Mandeberg, Howard Harrison, and Joseph Sahloff, were Air Group 88 fighter pilots on the US aircraft carrier *Yorktown* in the Pacific. The US had just dropped atomic bombs on Japan and everyone was sure Japan would surrender quickly. But until that happened, the war had to continue. On August 15, 1945, the four pilots flew their Hellcats outside Tokyo. Their job was to clear the way for bombers who were going to hit factories on the ground.

While the men were flying toward Tokyo, word came over the radio that Hirohito had agreed to a surrender. The planes were ordered to return to the ship. The war was over. The planes turned around and began to head back. The men were relieved and happy.

The Japanese planes in the area either had not heard about the surrender or didn't care. The American planes were set upon by at least 15 Japanese planes. The Americans shot down four of the Japanese planes, but the Japanese retaliated. Sahloff's plane was shot and he parachuted out but did not survive. The other three pilots were killed when their planes were shot. All four men died after finding out the war had ended.

Q: Which battleship was sent on a suicide mission?

A: The Japanese battleship *Yamato* was sent on a mission on April 6, 1945. The ship was sent to battle the Allied forces near Okinawa. However, the ship was sent out with only enough fuel for a one-way trip. It was a suicide mission with an intent to take out as many Allied ships as possible. The *Yamato* was sunk by bombs and torpedoes on April 7.

Q: Which Japanese plot was kept quiet by the American news media?

A: In 1944, the Japanese began launching balloon bombs. Called "Project Fugo," the balloons were handmade of paper created from tree bark. Each balloon carried a bomb. About 6,000 of the bombs were launched from Japan and carried by the air stream across the Pacific Ocean to the United States. The US government asked the news media not to report about the balloon bombs so that the Japanese would not know if they were successful. Only one explosion is known about. In early 1945, a woman and five children were killed in Oregon by a balloon bomb.

Q: How many bombs were dropped during the Battle of Dresden?

A: The Allies attacked Dresden, Germany, in February 1945. They used a tactic called area bombing. This meant they heavily bombed the entire city with the intent to destroy it. In the three-day campaign, 2,030 tons of high explosive bombs and 1,390 tons of incendiary (fire) bombs were dropped by the British and American planes. By the time the war was over, the entire city of Dresden was mostly destroyed. The city estimated that as many as 25,000 people were killed.

Q: Which battle from World War II made the *Guinness Book of World Records*?

A: On January 26, 1945, the British troops took Ramree Island near Myanmar. After the battle, there were 1,000 Japanese soldiers left. The British pushed the survivors into a mangrove swamp. The swamp was filled with saltwater crocodiles. Saltwater crocodiles can be as long as 20 feet and weigh up to 2,000 pounds each. The crocodiles attacked the fleeing soldiers. It's likely that the blood from the first few attacks drew even more crocodiles. Only 400 of the 1,000 Japanese soldiers made it out of the swamp. *The Guinness Book of World Records* calls this "The Most Number of Fatalities in a Crocodile Attack."

Q: What did General Patton do when he crossed the Rhine River in France for the first time?

A: According to reports of men who were there on March 1945, Patton urinated in the Rhine the first time he crossed it. This is reportedly something a lot of soldiers did on their first crossing.

Q: Who brought down a German observation plane using only pistols?

A: Lieutenant Duane Francies and Lieutenant Bill Martin, Americans, flew an unarmed Piper L-4 Grasshopper plane named *Miss Me*. Their job was just to do observation and report back. In April 1945 they were flying over Germany when they saw a German Fieseler Storch observation plane. This plane was also unarmed.

Francies and Martin shot at the plane with their pistols, damaging it enough that it was forced to land. They then captured the two Germans aboard it and flew them back to their troops. Since the Grasshopper has only two seats, it was probably a very crowded ride.

Q: Some Japanese survived the atom bombs at Nagasaki and Hiroshima, but did anyone survive both?

A: Yes. Engineer Tsutomu Yamaguchi was in Hiroshima on August 6, 1945, working on the design of an oil tanker, when the atom bomb was dropped there. He was less than two miles away from the bomb site and survived. He went to the train station, at one point swimming across a river filled with dead bodies. He took the train home to Nagasaki and went to the hospital there. He was treated and went home. On August 9 he went to work. He was telling his colleagues about what happened when the second bomb was dropped on Nagasaki. He was within two miles of the blast again. He survived both bombs. He later spoke about nuclear disarmament at the United Nations.

Q: Which American soldier saved 75 lives without ever touching a weapon?

A: Private First Class Desmond Doss was a conscientious objector. This meant he did not believe in using violence and he would not touch a weapon. He could have deferred (delayed) service when he was drafted but felt a moral obligation to help. He enlisted in the army as a medic. In 1945 he was present at the Battle of Okinawa. He ran through Japanese fire to rescue soldiers and brought back 75 of them without using a weapon to defend himself. Each time he brought one back, he asked God "help me get one more." Doss was awarded the Medal of Honor for his bravery and was the first conscientious objector to get this award.

Q: Did the Germans and Americans ever fight on the same side in the war?

A: On May 5, 1945, American forces were trying to liberate French prisoners of war held by the Nazis. The prisoners were in Castle Itter in the Austrian Alps. The prisoners were elderly French government officials, including two past premiers of France. Germany was close to surrender. The commander of the castle took his own life, and the guards at the castle fled.

The prisoners broke into the weapons room and took all the weapons they could find. However, the prisoners couldn't escape because there were German troops outside. The prisoners sent a man out to get a message to American troops asking for the help. He stole a bike and found a group of German soldiers who had deserted the German army. The commander of the German group sent him to where he knew the Americans were. The messenger found the Americans, but they were delayed in responding because of fighting along the way. However, the commander of the rogue German troops had also gone to find some Americans. He rode up to them flying a white surrender flag and told them about the French prisoners. The rogue Germans banded together with this small group of American soldiers and their one tank named Besotten Jenny. They made it into the castle and fought the loyal German forces from there. The rogue Germans, the Americans, and the French prisoners fought together. American tanks and more troops later arrived and won against the loyal German forces.

This was the only time Germans had fought on the same side as the Americans. Instead of being rewarded for their efforts, the rogue German forces were sent to a prisoner of war camp by the Americans.

Q: Why did a general order that a flag raised by troops be taken down during the Battle of Okinawa?

A: Many people are familiar with a photograph of an American flag being raised by US troops on Mount Suribachi on Iwo Jima in 1945. However, fewer people know that some soldiers wanted to fly the Confederate flag during the war. There are actually a few instances when American troops raised this flag. One instance happened during the Battle of Okinawa. Army Lieutenant General Simon Buckner Jr. ordered the flag be taken down and told his men, "Americans from all over are involved in this battle."

Q: Who was the youngest marine to receive the Medal of Honor?

A: Jacklyn "Jack" Lucas forged his mother's signature and joined the US Marines at age 14. The marines discovered the lie and assigned him to drive trucks in Hawaii. Lucas stowed away on a ship to Iwo Jima. When the marines found him, they let him join them. In February 1945 he landed on Iwo Jima and assisted in the fight. One Japanese grenade fell near him, and he threw himself on it

Private First Class Jacklyn H. Lucas, the youngest marine to receive the Medal of Honor

and shouted "grenade!" to warn the other men. A second grenade landed nearby, and he grabbed it and pulled it underneath him. One of them exploded. He was hit with more than 250 pieces of shrapnel. Everyone assumed he was dead until a passing marine saw he was alive. He was carried to the beach and waited there all day to be taken to a hospital ship. He had 26 surgeries. Eight months later he was recovered enough to walk to receive the Medal of Honor from President Truman. He was the youngest marine ever awarded this honor (he was 17 at the time).

Q: **When did the only submarine vs. submarine battle take place?**

A: In February 1945 the British sub HMS *Venturer* was off the coast of Norway and picked up via sonar the sound of a submarine with engine trouble. The German U-boat *U-864* was in the area and was heading back because it was having a problem with its engine. The captain of the *Venturer* tracked it using a hydrophone (a microphone in the water) instead of sonar, knowing that the sonar pings would be picked up by the German U-boat. When they were close enough, the *Venturer* fired four torpedoes. One of them hit the U-boat and sank it. This was the very first time and the only time a submarine has sunk another submarine.

Q: **After Germany surrendered, how did the US military decide which soldiers were sent to the Pacific?**

A: Once Germany surrendered, World War II shifted to be only a Pacific war. Some servicemen were left in Europe to occupy it. Others were sent to the Pacific. Some were lucky enough to go home. The military used a point system to decide who went where. A soldier needed 85 points to be able to go home. Here's how the points were awarded:

- 1 point for each month of service
- 1 point for each month they served overseas
- 5 points for each campaign they served in

- 5 points for a medal or a merit
- 5 points for a Purple Heart
- 12 points for each child they had at home, up to three children

Q: What new kind of submarine did the Japanese invent but never fully use?

A: In 1945, the Japanese launched a new class of submarines that were also aircraft carriers. The I-400 submarine could carry three Aichi M6A Seiran "Mountain Haze" planes in watertight hangars. The planes' wings had to be folded in for them to fit. Each sub was 400 feet long. None of them were used to launch planes. The subs were surrendered to the United States when the war ended.

Q: How did a submarine take down a train?

A: Submarines fight in the water. But one American submarine managed to take out a train on land. The USS *Barb* was in the Sea of Okhotsk off Japan in 1945. The crew could see Japanese trains running on land. They knew the trains carried troops and supplies, and they wanted to take them out. So the crew went to shore on rubber life rafts. They brought along the explosives they had on board, which were to be used to scuttle their own ship if it was attacked. They placed the explosives in an empty pickle can under the track. They set up a switch that would be triggered by the train going over the tracks. They blew up the train. This is the only case in which a submarine took out a train.

Q: What was the worst shark attack in history?

A: On July 30, 1945, the USS *Indianapolis* was hit by Japanese torpedoes and sank. There were 1,196 men on board and 900 survived the attack. Survivors floated in the water with life jackets.

Sharks ate the corpses and attacked those who were injured. The men huddled in groups and the sharks attacked those on the edges of the groups. Some men opened a can of Spam and the smell of the meat drew sharks near. After four days in the water, the survivors were rescued. Of the 900 who initially survived the attack, only 317 were left. This was the largest shark attack in history.

Q: Which pilot took another plane down using just his propeller?

A: On May 10, 1945, Marine pilot Bob Klingman was flying near Okinawa, Japan. The Japanese were sending up planes to take photographs from the sky of American naval forces. Klingman was in the air near one of these planes. He flew his plane so high that the guns on the plane froze and couldn't be fired. He flew his plane directly at the Japanese plane. First, he knocked off part of the rudder with his propeller. Then, he knocked the gunner and machine gun into the sky with his propeller. Finally, he broke the plane's tail using his propeller. The Japanese plane broke apart in the sky. Klingman made it back to the runway safely.

REFERENCES

WEBSITES

Air Force Historical Support Division
www.AFHistory.af.mil

Air & Space magazine
www.AirSpaceMag.com

History Channel
www.History.com

Naval History and Heritage Command
www.History.Navy.mil

US Marine Corps
www.Marines.mil

The National WWII Museum
www.nationalww2museum.org

Warefare History Network
www.WarfareHistoryNetwork.com

War History Online
www.WarHistoryOnline.com

We Are The Mighty
www.WeAreTheMighty.com

BOOKS

Bouverie, Tim. *Appeasement: Chamberlain, Hitler, Churchill and the Road to War.* New York: Tim Duggan Books, 2019.

Frank, Anne. *The Diary of a Young Girl.* New York: Bantam Books, 1993.

Gavin, Phillip. *World War II in Europe.* San Diego: Lucent Books, 2004.

Kershaw, Alex. *The First Wave: The D-Day Warriors Who Led the Way to Victory in World War II.* New York: Dutton Caliber, 2019.

Pyle, Ernie. *Here Is Your War: Story of G.I. Joe.* Lincoln, NE: Bison Books, 2004.

Taylor, Diane. *World War II: From the Rise of the Nazi Party to the Dropping of the Atom Bomb.* White River Junction, VT: Nomad Press, 2018.

DK. *World War II: Visual Encyclopedia.* London: DK Children, 2015.

PHOTO CREDITS

page 3: National Archives, ARC Identifier 535795

page 7: US Army

page 9: Wikimedia Commons

page 11: US Army

page 13: 80-G-14239 National Archives

page 14: 80-G-K-17386 National Archives

page 19: © Everett Collection/ shutterstock.com

page 21: Wikimedia Commons

page 27: National Archives, ARC Identifier 513210

page 29: Bundesarchiv, Bild 183-1987-1210-502 / Hoffmann, Heinrich / CC-BY-SA 3.0 / Wikimedia Commons

page 30: Wikimedia Commons

page 31: National Archives, ARC Identifier 197095

page 32: Wikimedia Commons

page 33: National Archives, ARC Identifier 559369

page 37: Wikimedia Commons

page 41: © Matt Gibson/ shutterstock.com

page 42: © Ben Brooksbank/ Wikimedia Commons

page 44: National Archives, ARC Identifier 535842

page 46: Wikimedia Commons

page 55: Library of Congress

page 56: 80-G-408456 National Archives

page 59: Air Force Historical Research Agency

page 62: Wikimedia Commons

page 66: National Archives, ARC Identifier 12009098

page 68: Wikimedia Commons

page 71: Naval History and Heritage Command Catalog #: USAF 22850 AC

page 72: Library of Congress

page 77: Air Force Historical Research Agency

page 80: National Archives, ARC Identifier 295175

page 82: 80-G-20683 National Archives

page 85: Library of Congress

page 88: NH 52362 Naval History and Heritage

page 89: SC 193146 National Archives

page 91: Naval History and Heritage Command Catalog #: NH 95561

page 92: 80-G-701378 National Archives

page 102: 80-G-44177 National Archives

page 105: Library of Congress

page 106: Wikimedia Commons

page 107: 80-G-270516 National Archives

page 110: © seeshooteatrepeat/ shutterstock.com

page 113: US Army

page 115: United States Coast Guard

page 121: Wikimedia Commons

page 123: Wikimedia Commons

page 125: National Archives, ARC Identifier 520748

page 126: US Air Force

page 127: Department of Defense

page 133: National Archives

page 139: NH 103872 Naval History and Heritage Command

ABOUT THE AUTHOR

Brette Sember is a former lawyer and the author of many books. Her titles include *The Everything Kids' Money Book* and *The Quiz Book 3: Three Times the Fun (American Girl Library)*. She lives in western New York State with her husband and two golden retrievers. Her web site is www.BretteSember.com.